CONCISE GUIDE TO
Psychodynamic Psychotherapy
*Principles and Techniques in the
Era of Managed Care*

Second Edition

Robert J. Ursano, M.D.,
Stephen M. Sonnenberg, M.D., and
Susan G. Lazar, M.D.

American
Psychiatric
Press, Inc.

Washington, DC
London, England

Note: The authors have worked to ensure that all information in this book concerning drug dosages, schedules, and routes of administration is accurate as of the time of publication and consistent with standards set by the U.S. Food and Drug Administration and the general medical community. As medical research and practice advance, however, therapeutic standards may change. For this reason and because human and mechanical errors sometimes occur, we recommend that readers follow the advice of a physician who is directly involved in their care or the care of a member of their family.

Copyright © 1998 American Psychiatric Press, Inc.
ALL RIGHTS RESERVED
Manufactured in the United States of America on acid-free paper
Second Edition
01 00 99 98   4 3 2 1

American Psychiatric Press, Inc.
1400 K Street, N.W., Washington, DC   20005
www.appi.org

Library of Congress Cataloging-in-Publication Data
Ursano, Robert J., 1947-
    Concise guide to psychodynamic psychotherapy : principles and techniques in the era of managed care / Robert J. Ursano, Stephen M. Sonnenberg, Susan G. Lazar. — 2nd ed.
        p.   cm. — (Concise guides / American Psychiatric Press)
    Includes bibliographical references and index.
    ISBN 0-88048-347-4 (alk. paper)
    1. Psychodynamic psychotherapy.   I. Sonnenberg, Stephen M., 1940-
. II. Lazar, Susan G., 1944-   .   III. Title.   IV. Series: Concise guides (American Psychiatric Press)
    [DNLM: 1. Psychotherapy—methods—handbooks.   WM 420 U82c 1998]
RC489.P72U77   1998
616.89′14—dc21
DNLM/DLC
for Library of Congress   97-25925
                                                                                              CIP

British Library Cataloguing in Publication Data
A CIP record is available from the British Library.

CONTENTS

About the Authors

Robert J. Ursano, M.D., is Professor and Chairman of the Department of Psychiatry at the Uniformed Services University of the Health Sciences, F. Edward Hébert School of Medicine, in Bethesda, Maryland. He is also on the teaching faculty of the Washington Psychoanalytic Institute in Washington, D.C.

Stephen M. Sonnenberg, M.D., is Clinical Professor in the Department of Psychiatry at the Uniformed Services University of the Health Sciences, F. Edward Hébert School of Medicine, in Bethesda, Maryland, and Clinical Professor in the Department of Psychiatry, Baylor College of Medicine, Houston, Texas. He is also Training and Supervising Analyst at the Houston-Galveston Psychoanalytic Institute, based in Austin, Texas.

Susan G. Lazar, M.D., is Clinical Professor in the Department of Psychiatry at the Uniformed Services University of the Health Sciences, F. Edward Hébert School of Medicine, in Bethesda, Maryland, and at the George Washington University School of Medicine, Washington, D.C. She is also Training and Supervising Analyst at the Washington Psychoanalytic Institute in Washington, D.C.

Introduction

to the *American Psychiatric Press Concise Guides*

The American Psychiatric Press Concise Guide series provides, in a most accessible format, practical information for psychiatrists and especially for psychiatry residents working in such varied treatment settings as inpatient psychiatry services, outpatient clinics, consultation-liaison services, and private practice. The Concise Guides are meant to complement the more detailed information to be found in lengthier psychiatry texts. The Concise Guides address topics of greatest concern to psychiatrists in clinical practice. The books in this series contain a detailed Table of Contents, along with an index, tables, and charts for easy access; and their size, designed to fit into a lab coat pocket, makes them a convenient source of information. The number of references has been limited to those most relevant to the material presented.

Drs. Ursano, Sonnenberg, and Lazar have prepared an outstanding summary of the major principles of psychodynamic psychotherapy in their *Concise Guide to Psychodynamic Psychotherapy.* The second edition has been thoroughly updated to include frequent references to psychotherapy practice in today's era of managed care. All the authors are members of the Department of Psychiatry at the Uniformed Services University of the Health Sciences, F. Edward Hébert School of Medicine; Dr. Ursano is Chairman of the Department. In addition, Dr. Ursano is at the Washington Psychoanalytic Institute in Washington, D.C.; Dr. Sonnenberg is with the Department of Psychiatry, Baylor College of Medicine, Houston, Texas, and the Houston-Galveston Psychoanalytic Institute, based in Austin, Texas; and Dr. Lazar is at George Washington University School of Medicine, Washington, D.C., and the Washington Psychoanalytic Institute in Washington, D.C. All three authors are well-respected and highly published experts in the field of psychodynamic psychotherapy.

The authors have prepared a wonderful review of the many issues that trainees and beginning therapists need to be familiar with in approaching psychodynamic psychotherapy. They have organized their book in a logical fashion that highlights key issues of particular relevance for the beginning psychotherapist.

The authors begin their book (Chapter 1) by answering the title question, "Why Psychotherapy?" and discuss issues related to the efficacy and cost effectiveness of psychotherapy—important issues in this era of managed care. In Chapter 2, they discuss basic principles: the focus, setting, and technique of psychodynamic psychotherapy. The authors have added several new chapters on the patient evaluation: assessment, diagnosis, and the prescription of psychotherapy (Chapter 3), psychodynamic listening (Chapter 4), and psychodynamic evaluation (Chapter 5).

The authors then discuss practical issues about beginning treatment with patients in psychodynamic psychotherapy (Chapter 6). They include information on educating patients as to what they may expect from the psychotherapeutic process. Also addressed are issues of abstinence and how the patient should be made aware that the therapist may become less verbally active as the treatment proceeds. The authors then turn to practical issues of safety and physicianly concern, and emphasize what the therapist's early experience may be concerning transference, defense, and resistance.

Four outstanding chapters that summarize the major issues in psychodynamic psychotherapy are then presented: resistance and defense (Chapter 7), transference (Chapter 8), countertransference (Chapter 9), and dreams (Chapter 10). Each of these chapters is well organized and provides a wealth of practical clinical suggestions for the beginning therapist. For instance, the authors provide guidance on how to interpret resistance and defense mechanisms, and they discuss the important topic of transference resistance. They also provide an excellent summary of the various forms of transference and countertransference and discuss in reasonable depth the use of dreams in the psychotherapeutic process.

Just as they start their book by discussing issues concerning beginning therapy, the authors have a separate chapter about termination (Chapter 11). Issues that are addressed in this chapter include how to recognize when the termination phase is approaching, the therapist's tasks for termination, how to identify whether treatment is unsuccessful, and what reactions the therapist may experience with termination. I was particularly pleased with the chapter entitled "Practical Problems and Their Management" (Chapter 12), in which a host of issues are discussed that are not commonly addressed in standard curricula: the office setting, fees, telephone calls, scheduling vacations, suicidal and dangerous patients, how to handle gifts, advice giving, illness in the patient, and what to do when the therapist makes errors.

The remaining three chapters focus on three related topics of great interest in psychodynamic psychotherapy: brief psychotherapy (Chapter 13), psychotherapy of borderline personality disorder and other severe character pathology (Chapter 14), and supportive psychotherapy (Chapter 15). With regard to brief psychodynamic psychotherapy and supportive psychotherapy, the authors discuss how to select patients for each of these treatment modalities and which techniques to employ. They also include additional readings to which the reader may turn for more information. In the chapter on the treatment of patients with borderline personality disorder, the authors discuss diagnostic issues, conflicts that may occur between the patient and the therapist, how to begin psychotherapy with these patients, countertransference issues, and how to work with a borderline patient's defenses. They also discuss particular issues in dealing with narcissistic and schizoid patients that may prove challenging for the therapist.

This truly outstanding book is especially useful for residents, medical students, and clinicians who want a brief review of psychodynamic psychotherapy. The authors have included many tables that summarize important points contained within each chapter and that highlight relevant clinical material. The book is written in clear, precise prose, with clinically relevant information contained throughout. The authors have shown a remarkable ability to integrate complex material in a coherent yet concise fashion. The second edition has been extensively revised to include many up-to-date references, as well as additional readings, to which the reader may wish to turn for further clarification.

Drs. Ursano, Sonnenberg, and Lazar have prepared a wonderful pocket-size book on psychodynamic psychotherapy that should be of great help to psychiatrists and other mental health professionals who use or want to learn to use this treatment modality.

Robert E. Hales, M.D.
Series Editor
American Psychiatric Press Concise Guides

Preface to the Second Edition

In the present-day world of multiple and complex treatments for psychiatric illness, the beginning therapist may not have as much psychoanalytic background as was the case in previous years. Yet, as a clinician, he or she may want to understand and use psychodynamic psychotherapy as a part of the therapeutic armamentarium and also use psychodynamic techniques in the evaluation and treatment of patients for whom a full psychotherapy may not be appropriate or may not be possible.

Developing skill in psychodynamic psychotherapy and its techniques is a lifetime endeavor. This treatment modality provides the clinician a window on the meaning of behaviors that are inexplicable from other vantage points. In addition, it requires the therapist to recognize patterns of interpersonal interaction without engaging in the "drama." In this process the psychotherapist comes to recognize and understand his or her own reactions as early indicators of events transpiring in the treatment and as potential roadblocks to a successful treatment. This knowledge and this skill are also applicable to other psychiatric treatment modalities, including the other psychotherapies, medication management, consultation-liaison psychiatry, outpatient and emergency room assessment and evaluation, and inpatient treatment.

In this concise guide the clinician is introduced to the concepts and techniques of psychoanalytic psychotherapy. In the present era of managed care and increasing cost consciousness, it is important that we also stay alert to the data on the efficacy and cost effectiveness of psychotherapy and psychodynamic psychotherapy in particular. We have included a review of this area in Chapter 1, "Why Psychotherapy?" the question often asked in the cost-conscious world of present psychiatric care. In addition, it is increasingly important to recognize the basic skills and techniques of psychodynamic intervention that are used in treatments other than psychotherapy. Psychodynamic listening and psychodynamic evaluation are two such techniques, which are best learned in the context of learning psychodynamic psychotherapy but are applied in many other psychiatric diagnostic, treatment, and prediction methods.

We believe this volume will benefit those who seek the most helpful treatments for the pain and suffering of their patients with psychiatric illness. We hope that it will convey the excitement and the usefulness—as well as the difficulties—of psychodynamic psychotherapy and its techniques.

Robert J. Ursano, M.D.
Stephen M. Sonnenberg, M.D.
Susan G. Lazar, M.D.

WHY PSYCHOTHERAPY?

Psychotherapy has long been a part of the treatment of psychiatric patients. Clinical experience, and increasingly empirical research as well, have shown psychotherapy to be both efficacious and cost effective. The effectiveness of psychotherapy can be presented in several ways. A reevaluation of a classic study by Eysenck indicates that psychotherapy accomplishes in 15 sessions what spontaneous remission takes 2 years to do (1). Smith and colleagues found an average effect size of 0.68; this means that after treatment, the average treated person was better off than 75% of the untreated sample (2, 3). The effect size found by Smith and colleagues is larger than the effect sizes for some other medical treatment trials; these trials were stopped before completion because the data indicated the treatment was efficacious enough that it would be unethical to withhold treatment (4). Similarly, such effect sizes are the equivalent of a surgeon's saying that with the surgery, 66% will survive, and without it, only 34% will survive (5). Is there any question about whether to have such a surgery? Similar effect sizes have been found for psychodynamic psychotherapy in particular (6).

We often must remind ourselves, as well as other physicians and health policy makers, that psychiatric illness is not uncommon. There are psychiatric "common colds" as well as psychiatric "cancers." Often we forget the range of psychiatric illnesses and therefore the range of interventions—including psychotherapy—that are needed when one considers community health needs as a whole. Because of this range of psychiatric disorders and their effects on health, there appears to be substantial economic advantage in including psychotherapy benefits in all health insurance plans, not only for those with primary psychiatric illness, but also for those with medical illness and accompanying psychiatric problems.

■ PSYCHIATRIC ILLNESS

In the United States, nearly 50% of the noninstitutionalized adult population have a psychiatric disorder at some point in their lifetime, although less than 50% of sufferers from psychiatric illness ever receive any treatment (7). Of those who do seek care for psychiatric illness, only one-third are seen by mental health care providers. We often forget that anxiety disorders are the most prevalent psychiatric illness, affecting 17% of adults yearly and 25% over a lifetime. Affective disorders have a lifetime prevalence of 19%, major depression being the most common at 17%. Nearly 40% of urban residents experience severe trauma, and one-quarter of the 40% develop posttraumatic stress disorder (PTSD) (8). The problems of our children are also substantial. Mood disorders affect 17% of children (9). The prevalence of major depression in adolescents is 4% and of dysthymia 5% (10). Suicide is the second leading cause of death in adolescent males (11). The cost of mental illness and substance abuse has been estimated to be $273 billion per year (12), including treatment costs, law enforcement costs, mortality, and decreased productivity. One study has estimated that the annual cost of depression alone is $43.7 billion (13).

■ THE CONTRIBUTION OF PSYCHOTHERAPY

Psychotherapy is essential to the care of many diagnostic groups of psychiatric patients. It can be crucial for many depressed patients, especially for those who cannot take antidepressant medication, such as pregnant and nursing mothers, some elderly depressed patients, and some depressed patients with concomitant medical illnesses. Whereas antidepressants improve the neurovegetative symptoms of depression, psychotherapy improves the interpersonal and self-esteem symptoms (14, 15). Even as little as once-monthly interpersonal psychotherapy as a maintenance treatment can prevent recurrence of major depression for nearly twice as long as placebos (16). Extended psychotherapy is often also a crucial treatment for the half of depressed patients who develop work impairments, which require a more extended course of treatment—psychotherapy, medication, or a combined treatment approach (17). Recent studies have indicated that extended dynamic psychotherapy is more efficacious for perfectionistic depressed patients than are other treatment approaches, including medication (18). Studies from the Anna Freud Centre have demonstrated that more intensive psychotherapy is effective for child patients with severe depression, personality disorders, and anxiety disorders (19). Because antidepressant medication often does not have its usual effectiveness with adolescent patients, psychotherapy can be especially important for depressed adolescents (20).

Patients with PTSD benefit from psychotropic medication for their symptoms of numbing and alienation. However, extended psychotherapy can be helpful in restoring work and interpersonal functioning (21). Recent research has demonstrated a need for at least 1 year and preferably $2\frac{1}{2}$ years of intensive psychotherapy for borderline patients. This can result in increased work functioning and decreased suicidality, medical costs, psychiatric hospitalization, and emergency room visits for this most difficult group of patients (22–26). One study has also shown that borderline patients require a longer course of psychotherapy than do anxious and depressed patients before they begin to improve (27). Patients with multiple personality disorder also frequently have a history of early life abuse and trauma. One researcher (28) has documented the need for twice-weekly psychotherapy for at least $2\frac{1}{2}$ years to resolve the personality fragmentation and a need for ongoing treatment beyond this point. These patients can have a great reduction in the medical costs of hospitalization after extended psychotherapy (28). Patients with schizophrenia also benefit from psycho-therapy. Family psychotherapy in particular has been demon-strated to be highly cost-effective in that it leads to decreased relapse and hospitalization. One study found a cost-benefit ratio (calculated as treatment costs : savings in hospitalization) of 1:17 for single-family psychotherapy and 1:34 for multiple-family psychotherapy (29).

■ PSYCHOTHERAPY AND MEDICAL ILLNESS

Medical and surgical patients are at particular risk of psychiatric illness. They may, therefore, need specific psychotherapeutic treat-ment. Medical and surgical patients have a higher incidence of anxiety and depression than does the rest of the population. Eleven percent of medical inpatients and 6% of patients in primary care settings have major depression (30). Half of all cancer patients have a psychiatric illness. One year of dynamic psychotherapy has been shown to ameliorate nausea, pain, depression, and anxiety in metastatic breast cancer patients and has been reported to lead to a substantially increased survival rate (31). Briefer psychotherapy has been related to increased survival in malignant melanoma patients (32, 33). Similarly, diabetic children given three- to four-times-weekly psychotherapy during a 15-week hospitalization have a much stabler medical course afterward than do control-group patients not given psychotherapy (34).

Poorly adjusted medical patients have nearly double the medi-cal costs of well-adjusted patients (35). Studies have shown that brief psychotherapeutic interventions from consultation-liaison services lead to decreased medical costs for patients with somati-zation disorder (36), for older patients with hip fractures (37), and for depressed medical patients (38) (Table 1–1). In one study of selected groups of patients with chronic disease, outpatient psy-chotherapy was shown to reduce medical costs (39). Another study demonstrated a 10%–33% overall medical cost saving after pa-tients were given psychotherapy (40). The fact that psychotherapy

Table 1–1.   **Benefits of psychotherapy**

Effective treatment; efficacy similar to that of many medical treatments

Part of the medical armamentarium available for treatment of a range of disorders

Targets treatment of interpersonal and behavioral symptoms

Complementary to psychopharmacological treatment

Treatment of choice in some psychiatric disorders

Decreases overall cost of hospitalizations

can have such dramatic effects on both the emotional and the physical well-being of medical patients becomes less surprising when one considers the mounting evidence for mind-body interactions. The research of Baxter et al. demonstrated that the positron-emission tomography (PET) scan changes in the brains of obsessive-compulsive patients were similar after treatment with psychotherapy and after treatment with the drug fluoxetine hydrochloride (41).

Several large actuarial studies have strongly implied the cost savings realized by providing psychotherapy as medically necessary. Australia, with readily available outpatient psychotherapy, has a mental health care delivery system with a 44% lower per capita cost than New Zealand, with its hospital-based system and little outpatient treatment (42). A study of the U.S. military services' CHAMPUS system (the insurance program for retirees and military dependents) demonstrated a savings in hospital costs of $4 for every extra $1 spent on expanded outpatient psychotherapy (43).

Three percent of the American public has had some outpatient psychotherapy. Patients who have been in long-term psychotherapy (more than 20 sessions) were also found to be more distressed, to be in poorer general health, to have higher general medical costs, to have more impairment, and to be more likely to have had psychotropic medication and psychiatric hospitalization (44). This finding suggests that these patients are in treatment as a result of overwhelming need and not, as has been suggested, in an attempt to take advantage of an overly generous insurance benefit. Nonetheless, even when insurance coverage for psychotherapy is free, only 4.3% of the covered population uses it, and the average length of treatment is 11 sessions (45).

In summary, psychotherapy is a powerful and effective medical treatment modality. (For a more extensive review of this information, see reference 46.) For a number of psychiatric patient groups, it is a necessary treatment; for certain medical and surgical patients, it can improve and perhaps extend life. Furthermore, current data indicate that psychotherapy is a substantial tool in our efforts to contain medical costs in general and the expense of psychiatric hospitalization in particular. In our present cost-conscious climate, psychotherapy should be supported as a part of all medical insurance policies and public service medical care plans. Data on the specific and differential effects of various types of psychotherapy are generally limited and probably will not be available for some time, given the complicated nature of such studies when well performed. However, available data on long-term psychodynamic psychotherapy with some diagnostic groups, on brief psychodynamic psychotherapy, on interpersonal psychotherapy derived from psychodynamic psychotherapy, and on supportive psychotherapy derived from the application of psychodynamic principles indicate that psychodynamic psychotherapy is an important, valuable, and cost-effective part of the clinician's armamentarium. Skills in this modality should be an important part of every clinician's training and intervention skills. This volume can serve as a beginning in gaining these skills.

■ REFERENCES

1. McNeilly CL, Howard KI: The effects of psychotherapy: a reevaluation based on dosage. Psychotherapy Research 1: 74–78, 1991
2. Smith ML, Glass GV, Miller TI: The Benefits of Psychotherapy. Baltimore, MD, Johns Hopkins University Press, 1980

3. Sonnenberg SM, Sutton L, Ursano RJ: Physician-patient relationship, in Psychiatry. Edited by Tasman A, Kaye J, Lieberman J. Philadelphia, PA: WB Saunders, 1996, pp 41–49

4. Rosenthal R: How are we doing in soft psychology? Am Psychol 45:775–777, 1990

5. Rosenthal R, Rubin DB: A simple, general-purpose display of magnitude of experimental effect. Journal of Educational Psychology 74:166–169, 1982

6. Crits-Christoph P: The efficacy of brief dynamic psychotherapy: a meta-analysis. Am J Psychiatry 149:151–158, 1992

7. Kessler R, McGonagle K, Zhao S, et al: Lifetime and 12-month prevalence of DSM-III-R psychiatric disorders in the United States. Arch Gen Psychiatry 51:8–19, 1994

8. Breslau N, Davis G, Andreski P, et al: Traumatic events and posttraumatic stress disorder in an urban population of young adults. Arch Gen Psychiatry 48:216–222, 1991

9. Kashani J, Simonds J: The incidence of depression in children. Am J Psychiatry 136:1203–1205, 1979

10. Whitaker A, Johnson J, Shaffer D: Uncommon troubles in young people: prevalence estimates of selected psychiatric disorders in a nonreferred adolescent population. Arch Gen Psychiatry 47:487–496, 1990

11. Centers for Disease Control: Suicide Surveillance, 1970–1980. Atlanta, GA, U.S. Department of Health and Human Services, Public Health Service, 1986

12. Rice D, Kelman S, Miller L, et al: Report on the economic costs of alcohol and drug abuse and mental illness: 1985. Washington, DC, U.S. Department of Health and Human Services, Public Health Service, Alcohol, Drug Abuse and Mental Health Administration, 1990

13. Greenberg P, Stiglin L, Finklestein S, et al: The economic burden of depression in 1990. J Clin Psychiatry 54:405–418, 1993

14. Klerman G, DiMascio A, Weissman M, et al: Treatment of depression by drugs and psychotherapy. Am J Psychiatry 131:186–191, 1974

15. DiMascio A, Weissman M, Prusoff B, et al: Differential symptom reduction by drugs and psychotherapy in acute depression. Arch Gen Psychiatry 36:1450–1456, 1979

16. Frank E, Kupfer D, Wagner E, et al: Efficacy of interpersonal psychotherapy as a maintenance treatment of recurrent depression: contributing factors. Arch Gen Psychiatry 48:1053–1059, 1991

17. Mintz J, Mintz L, Arruda M, et al: Treatments of depression and the functional capacity to work. Arch Gen Psychiatry 49:761–768, 1992

18. Blatt S, Quinlan D, Pilkonis P, et al: Impact of perfectionism and need for approval on the brief treatment of depression: the National Institute of Mental Health Treatment of Depression Collaborative Research Program revisited. J Consult Clin Psychol 63:125–132, 1995

19. Target M, Fonagy P: Efficacy of psychoanalysis for children with emotional disorders. J Am Acad Child Adolesc Psychiatry 33:361–371, 1994

20. Ryan N: The pharmacologic treatment of child and adolescent depression. Psychiatr Clin North Am 15:29–40, 1992

21. Lindy J: Presentation to the Mental Health Work Group of the White House Task Force for National Health Care Reform. Unpublished manuscript, Washington, DC, 1993

22. Linehan M, Armstrong H, Suarez A: Cognitive-behavioral treatment of chronically parasuicidal borderline patients. Arch Gen Psychiatry 48:1060–1064, 1991

23. Linehan M, Heard H, Armstrong H: Naturalistic follow-up of a behavioral treatment for chronically parasuicidal borderline patients. Arch Gen Psychiatry 50:971–974, 1993

24. Heard H: Behavior therapies for borderline patients. Paper presented at the 147th annual meeting of the American Psychiatric Association, Philadelphia, PA, May 21–26, 1994

25. Stevenson J, Meares R: An outcome study of psychotherapy for patients with borderline personality disorder. Am J Psychiatry 149:358–362, 1992

26. Hoke L: Longitudinal pattern of behavior in borderline personality disorder. Unpublished doctoral dissertation, Boston University, 1989

27. Howard K, Kopta S, Krause M, et al: The dose-effect relationship in psychotherapy. Am Psychol 41:159–164, 1986

28. Kluft R: The postunifiaction treatment of multiple personality disorder. Am J Psychother 42:212–228, 1988

29. McFarlane W, Lukens E, Link B: Multiple-family groups and psycheducation in the treatment of schizophrenia. Arch Gen Psychiatry 52:679–687, 1995

30. Katon W, Sullivan M: Depression and chronic medical illness. J Clin Psychiatry 56 (suppl):3–11, 1990

31. Spiegel D, Bloom J, Kraemer H, et al: Effect of psychsocial treatment on survival of patients with metastatic breast cancer. Lancet 2:888-891, 1989

32. Fawzy F, Kemeny M, Fawzy N, et al: A structured psychiatric intervention for cancer patients, II: changes over time in immunological measures. Arch Gen Psychiatry 47:729–735, 1990

33. Fawzy F, Fawzy N, Hyun C, et al: Malignant melanoma. Arch Gen Psychiatry 50:681–689, 1993

34. Moran G, Fonagy P, Kurt A, et al: A controlled study of the psychoanalytic treatment of brittle diabetes. J Am Acad Child Adolesc Psychiatry 30:926–935, 1991

35. Browne G, Arpin K, Corey P, et al: Individual correlates of health service utilization and the cost of poor adjustment to chronic illness. Med Care 28:43–58, 1990

36. Smith G, Monson R, Ray D: Psychiatric consultation in somatization disorder. N Engl J Med 314:1407–1413, 1986

37. Strain J, Lyons S, Hammer J, et al: Cost offset from a psychiatric consultation-liaison intervention with elderly hip fracture patients. Am J Psychiatry 148:1044–1049, 1991

38. Verbosky L. Franco K, Zrull J: The relationship between depression and length of stay in the general hospital patient. J Clin Psychiatry 54:177–181, 1993

39. Schlesinger H, Mumford E, Glass G, et al: Mental health treatment and medical care utilization in a fee-for-service system. Am J Public Health 73:422–429, 1983

40. Mumford E, Schlesinger H, Glass G, et al: A new look at evidence about reduced cost of medical utilization following mental health treatment. Am J Psychiatry 141:1145–1158, 1984

41. Baxter C, Schwartz S, Berman, K, et al: Caudate glucose metabolic rate changes with both drug and behavior therapy for obsessive-compulsive disorder. Arch Gen Psychiatry 49:681–689, 1992

42. Andrews G: Private and public psychiatry. Am J Psychiatry 146:881–886, 1989

43. Zients A: Presentation to the Mental Health Work Group of the White House Task Force for National Health Care Reform. Unpublished manuscript, Washington, DC, 1993

44. Olfson M, Pincus H: Outpatient psychotherapy in the United States, I: volume, costs and user characteristics. Am J Psychiatry 151:1281–1288, 1994

45. Manning W, Wells K, Duan N, et al: How cost sharing affects the use of ambulatory mental health services. JAMA 256:1930–1934, 1986

46. Lazar SG (ed): Extended dynamic psychotherapy: making the case in an era of managed care. Psychoanalytic Inquiry, Special Supplement, 1997

2

BASIC PRINCIPLES

Behavior, which includes thoughts, feelings, fantasies, and actions, has both direct and indirect effects on health. Psychiatric illnesses are behavioral disturbances that result in increased levels of morbidity and mortality. Psychopathology usually limits the individual's ability to see options and exercise choice. Feelings, thoughts, and actions are frequently restricted, painful, and repetitive. Psychotherapy, the "talking cure," is the medical treatment directed to changing behavior through verbal means. Through talk, psychotherapy provides understanding, support, and new experiences that can result in learning. The goal of all psychotherapies is to increase the range of behaviors available to the patient and, in this way, to relieve symptoms and alter patterns that have created increased morbidity and potential mortality.

A broad and comprehensive view of health and disease is needed in order to understand the relationship between behavior and health. The target organ of psychotherapeutic treatment is the brain. Feelings, thoughts, and behavior are basic brain functions. Therefore, if psychotherapy is to change behavior, it must at some basic level alter brain function and organization (1, 2). If a particular behavior is the result of neuron A firing to neuron B, then, if change is to occur, neuron A must now fire to neuron C. This simplistic example underscores the importance of recognizing the complex biological results of psychotherapeutic work.

Behavioral change can be the result of direct biological effects at the brain level (e.g., toxins, tumors), the unfolding of biology in maturation, or the effect of past and present life experiences interacting with biological givens. Psychotherapy itself is a life experience and can become a means by which what is "outside" changes what is "inside." Our understanding of the basic sciences of this process—how what is outside affects what is inside—is only now emerging (3). Recall, for example, when you last looked at a gestalt diagram, such as the one of the beautiful woman–ugly witch. At first, perhaps the beautiful woman was the only clear image. But after certain shaded areas were pointed out, it was possible to discern the chin of a witch rather than the face of the beautiful woman. Nothing had changed in the amount of visual information that was reaching your brain; rather, what changed was how it was organized, allowing a fuller range of meanings to be experienced and behaviors to be expressed.

A wide array of infant systems (activity level, arousal, and brain neurochemistry) are regulated by the mother-infant interaction and can be profoundly affected by it (4). In adults, also, the extent of social relatedness has been repeatedly shown to affect behavior as well as morbidity and mortality (5). For example, it is a common observation that the phobic patient will frequently approach the phobic object when with a supportive other. Why? How has the presence of another person altered brain function to allow this profound yet everyday change in behavior? Mental, symbolic, and representational events—including hopes, fears, memories, expectations, and fantasies—also serve as important biological regulators in the same way as do actual life events.

Our understanding of how the outside world (psychotherapy) can change the inside world (biology) is growing but is still in its infancy. Our basic sciences of psychotherapy have changed the question from *whether* organization, meaning, memory, expectations, and interpersonal contact influence health and behavior to *how* they influence them and to what extent.

■ THE FOCUS OF PSYCHODYNAMIC PSYCHOTHERAPY

The different psychotherapies target for change different aspects of psychological functioning. Psychodynamic (psychoanalytically oriented) psychotherapy focuses primarily on the effects of past experience on molding patterns of behavior through particular cognitions (defenses) and interpersonal styles of interaction and perception (transference) that have become repetitive and that interfere with health (see Table 2–1).

An individual's past exists in the present through memory and biology. Expectations, the anticipated present and future, are formed by one's past experiences and biology. Likewise, the way in which language is used metaphorically by a patient may reflect a particular organization (cluster of feelings, thoughts, and behaviors) formed in the past and affecting present perception and behavior. By exploring the past and present meaning of events and their context, the psychodynamic psychotherapist aims to alter the

---

TABLE 2–1.   **Psychodynamic psychotherapy**

Focus

The effects of past experience on present behaviors (cognitions, affects, fantasies, and actions)

Goal

Understanding the defense mechanisms and transference responses of the patient, particularly as they appear in the doctor-patient relationship

Technique

Therapeutic alliance

Free association

Defense and transference interpretation

Frequent meetings

Duration of treatment

Months to years

---

organizers of behavior, restructuring how information and experience are organized.

Psychodynamic psychotherapy (also called psychoanalytic psychotherapy, exploratory psychotherapy, or insight-oriented psychotherapy) is a method of treatment for psychiatric disorders that uses verbal exchange to effect changes in behavior. Psychodynamic psychotherapy shares with the other psychotherapies a general definition: a two-person interaction, primarily verbal, in which one person is designated the help giver and the other the help receiver. The goal is to elucidate the patient's characteristic problems of living; the hope is to achieve behavioral change. Psychodynamic psychotherapy uses specific techniques and a particular understanding of mental functioning to guide and direct the treatment and the therapist's interventions. As in other medical treatments, there are both indications and contraindications to this form of treatment.

Although the strategic goals of a psychodynamic treatment are to alter symptoms and change behavior to alleviate pain and suffering and decrease morbidity and mortality, the moment-to-moment objective is very different. As in surgery, where the strategic goal is to remove disease, stop bleeding, and eliminate pain, it is not these strategic goals that direct the actual operation itself. The surgeon sometimes causes bleeding and pain and is directed by technical procedures to accomplish the overall goal. Similarly, in psychodynamic psychotherapy it is the therapist's understanding of what is causing the disease process, and of how a particular intervention will effect the recovery in the long run, that directs the tactical moment-to-moment process of treatment.

Psychodynamic psychotherapy is based on the principles of mental functioning and the psychotherapeutic techniques originally developed by Sigmund Freud. Freud began his work by using hypnosis; he later turned to free association as the method by which to understand the unrecognized (unconscious) conflicts that arose from development and continued into adult life. Such conflicts are patterns of behavior—that is, patterns of feelings, thoughts, and behaviors laid down in the brain during childhood. These patterns are the result of the individual's developmental history and biological givens.

Typically, these unconscious conflicts are between libidinal or aggressive desires (wishes) and the fear of loss, the fear of retaliation, the limits imposed by the real world, or the opposition of conflicting desires. Libidinal wishes are best thought of as longings for sexual and emotional gratification. Aggressive wishes, on the other hand, are destructive wishes that either are primary or are the result of perceived frustration or deprivation (6). The beginning therapist frequently confuses the old terminology of *libidinal wishes* with the idea of specifically genital feelings. *Sexual gratification* in psychodynamic work refers to the broad concept of bodily pleasure—the states of excitement and pleasure experienced since infancy. The patient talking about happiness, excitement, pleasure, anticipation, love, or longing is describing libidinal wishes. The desire to destroy or the experience of pleasure in anger, hate, and pain is usually the expression of aggressive wishes.

Neurotic conflict can result in anxiety, depression, and somatic symptoms; work, social, or sexual inhibitions; or maladaptive interpersonal relations. These unconscious neurotic conflicts are evident as patterns of behavior: feelings, thoughts, fantasies, and actions. These patterns, learned in childhood, may at one time have been appropriate to the patient's childhood view of the world and may have been adaptive or even necessary for survival. Even though these behaviors are not evident to the patient initially, through the psychotherapeutic work they become clear and their many ramifications for the patient's life become evident.

Psychodynamic psychotherapy is usually more focused than a psychoanalysis per se and somewhat more oriented to the here and now. However, both these techniques share the goal of understanding the nature of the patient's conflicts—maladaptive patterns of behavior derived from childhood (also called the *infantile neurosis*)—and their effects in adult life.

■ THE SETTING OF PSYCHODYNAMIC PSYCHOTHERAPY

Psychodynamic psychotherapy may be brief (see Chapter 13, this volume) or long-term. The treatment may take from months to years. Typically, a longer-term treatment is open ended; no termination date is set in the beginning of treatment. The length of treatment depends on the number of conflict areas to be addressed and the course of the treatment. Psychotherapy sessions are usually held one, two, or three times a week, although in brief treatments once a week is the norm. The frequent meetings permit a more detailed exploration of the patient's inner life and a fuller development of the transference. The frequent meetings also support the patient during the treatment process. Medications are used as an adjunct to treatment to alleviate persistent and impairing symptoms and to allow a fuller range of affect to be experienced. In some cases, medication may alleviate a primary disease process so that the psychotherapy can address the illness-onset conditions and facilitate the patient's readjustment, recovery, and integration into family and community to decrease the risk of morbidity and mortality. The meaning to the patient of the medication he or she may be taking is an important area for exploration during the psychotherapy, particularly when it is time to discontinue use of the medication.

■ THE TECHNIQUE OF PSYCHODYNAMIC PSYCHOTHERAPY

Behavioral change occurs in psychodynamic psychotherapy primarily through two processes of treatment: understanding the cognitive and affective patterns derived from childhood (defense mechanisms) and understanding the conflicted relationship(s) one had with one's childhood significant figures as they are reexperienced in the doctor-patient relationship (transference). The recovery and understanding of these feelings and perceptions are the focus of treatment. The treatment setting is designed to facilitate the emergence of these patterns in a way that allows them to be analyzed rather than being confused with the reality of the doctor-patient relationship or being dismissed as trivial.

Primary to the success of psychoanalytically oriented psychotherapy is the need for the patient to feel engaged in the work and to trust the relationship with the therapist. This therapeutic alliance is built on the reality-based elements of the treatment, such as the mutual working together toward a common goal and the consistency and reliability of the therapist. Only in contrast to a good therapeutic alliance can the patient view the transference feelings and experience the distortion that the transference reveals.

It is most important for the clinician to hear empathically what the patient is trying to say and to understand what this means to the patient. What the patient is able to bring into focus is what is dealt with in the treatment (7). The depth of interpretation and exploration is always at the point of urgency for the patient, not ahead of, or behind, the patient's thoughts and feelings. Beginning therapists often think that as soon as they see something, it is time to tell the patient. Not so. The timing of when to tell the patient is the essence of the skill of the therapist; careful thought and planning are needed to determine when. Although the actual event of interpreting—explaining a piece of behavior in the context of the present and past and in relation to transference elements—is spontaneous, it is "spontaneous" after much preparation. When to tell the patient a new piece of information is determined by when the patient can hear and understand what the therapist has to say.

The patient's free association is encouraged. This encouragement can be as simple as telling a patient that she is free to talk about whatever she wishes. The therapist's main task is to listen to the undercurrents of the patient's associations. Frequently this involves wondering about the connection between one vignette and the next, or listening for how the patient is experiencing a particular person she describes or a particular interaction with the therapist. Often, listening to the ambiguity in a patient's associations may open the door to the unconscious conflict and the person from the past to whom it relates.

> For example, one patient came into a psychotherapy session shortly after breaking up with his girlfriend, saying, "I want to get her back." If one hears the double meaning in the sentence—to be back with her or to take revenge on her—it will not be surprising to learn that although the patient thought he was only talking about wanting to get back together with his girlfriend, by the end of the session he was describing his particular revenge fantasy. (This patient's fantasy derived from an old movie. He fantasized about "smushing" a grapefruit in his girlfriend's face.) The conflicted feelings—longing for and hating—were foretold in the opening of the session. This long-held pattern of response to rejections matched his early experiences with a mother who would alternately see him as having exactly the same feelings as she did and later chase him with a knife. He was not yet ready to hear this connection, but it was already becoming evident. The pattern could now be watched, and the patient's awareness of it slowly increased.

The transference may be experienced by the therapist as a pressure to act in a certain way toward the patient. More often than not, for the beginning therapist it is identified, as in learning to ski, by noticing the direction one is about to fall! The transference is a specific example of the tendency of the brain to see the past in the present, to make use of old patterns of perception and response, and to exclude new information. When the transference is alive, it is very real to the patient, and contradictory information is disregarded. For the new therapist it is often difficult to see the irrational elements in the patient's feelings and perceptions about the therapist. Often the transference is built on a seed of accurate perception about the therapist. It is the elaboration of this seed that makes the unconscious evident. The therapist may experience the accuracy of the patient's perceptions and fail to listen to the elements of the past that may be appearing.

Exploring the transference is just a special case of the ongoing work of examining the patterns of relationships that the patient experiences. This is all part of the attempt to understand the inner world of the patient—the world of how the patient sees and experiences people and events, the world of psychic reality. Transference is not unique to the psychotherapeutic setting. It occurs throughout life and in medical treatments of all kinds. In fact, asking someone to come into a hospital (an unfamiliar setting)—and take off his clothes, have no one know who he is, and be required to eat when told and go where told—is a very powerful way to induce transferences! What is unique is the attempt to understand the transference and to examine it when it occurs rather than to try to undo it.

The therapist may also experience feelings toward the patient that come from the therapist's past. This is called the *countertransference*. The countertransference is increased during times of stressful events and unresolved conflicts in the life of the therapist. The countertransference can be a friend, guiding one to see subtle aspects of the doctor-patient relationship that may have gone unnoticed although not unexperienced. It can also be a block to a successful treatment, causing the therapist to misperceive and mishear the patient.

■ **REFERENCES**

1. Kandell ER: Psychotherapy and the single synapse: the impact of psychiatric thought on neurobiologic research. N Engl J Med 301:1028–1037, 1979
2. Kandell ER: Genes, nerve cells, and the remembrance of things past. Journal of Neuropsychiatry 1:103–125, 1989
3. Ursano RJ, Fullerton CS: Psychotherapy: medical intervention and the

concept of normality, in Normality: Context and Theory. Edited by
Offer D, Sabshin M. New York, Basic Books, 1991, pp 39–59

4. Hofer MA: Relationships as regulators: psychobiologic perspective on
bereavement. Psychosom Med 46:183–197, 1984

5. House JS, Landis KR, Umberson D: Social relationships and health.
Science 241:540–545, 1988

6. Ursano RJ, Silberman EK, Diaz A Jr: The psychotherapies: basic
theoretical principles, techniques and indications, in Clinical Psychiatry for Medical Students. Edited by Stoudemire A. New York, JB
Lippincott, 1990, pp 855–890

7. Coleman JV: Aims and conduct of psychotherapy. Arch Gen Psychiatry
18:1–6, 1968

■ ADDITIONAL READINGS

Bruch H: Learning Psychotherapy: Rationale and Ground Rules. Cambridge, MA, Harvard University Press, 1974

Fromm-Reichmann F: Principles of Intensive Psychotherapy. Chicago, IL,
University of Chicago Press, 1950

Gabbard G: Psychodynamic Psychiatry in Clinical Practice: The DSM-IV
Edition. Washington, DC, American Psychiatric Press, 1994

Luborsky L: Principles of Psychoanalytic Psychotherapy: A Manual for
Supportive Expressive Treatment. New York, Basic Books, 1984

Luborsky L,Crits-Christoph P:Understanding Transference: The CCRT
Method. New York, Basic Books, 1990

Miller N, Luborsky L, Barber JP, et al (eds): Psychodynamic Treatment
Research: A Handbook for Clinical Practice. New York, Basic Books,
1993

Reiser MF: Mind, Brain, and Body: Toward a Convergence of Psychoanalysis and Neurobiology. New York, Basic Books, 1984

Strupp H, Binder J: Psychotherapy in a New Key. New York, Basic Books,
1984

Sullivan HS: The Psychiatric Interview. New York. WW Norton, 1954

3

PATIENT EVALUATION, I: ASSESSMENT, DIAGNOSIS, AND THE PRESCRIPTION OF PSYCHOTHERAPY

Psychiatric evaluation is critical to the assessment of a patient for psychotherapy, as much as or more than for the patient who is to be seen for medication management (1). The prescription of psychotherapy can be the outcome of the psychiatric evaluation, and the therapist must be as detailed in his or her thinking about advantages, disadvantages, target symptoms, course of treatment, and contraindications as with any other prescription. As part of the evaluation for psychodynamic psychotherapy, the clinician must assess the presence or absence of organic causes for the patient's psychiatric disturbance, the need for medication, the risk of untoward outcomes (suicide, homicide, divorce, work disruption), and the possibility that the patient's condition will worsen. At times, the beginning therapist, starting to work on a busy outpatient service, may neglect to consider the option that the patient assigned for psychotherapy was evaluated incorrectly, and that individual psychodynamic psychotherapy is not the appropriate treatment, or that no treatment is indicated.

In addition to asking questions of the patient—typical of all medical evaluations—the psychiatric assessment for psychodynamic psychotherapy includes the use of two important techniques: psychodynamic listening and the psychodynamic evaluation. These are described in greater detail in the following two chapters.

Both psychodynamic listening and psychodynamic evaluation are important to distinguish as techniques because they are applicable to many types of treatment and intervention, not only to psychodynamic psychotherapy. The use of psychodynamic listening and evaluation can be critical in medication management, consultation-liaison evaluation, and inpatient treatment, to name a few. This principle is particularly important to recall in the current era of managed care, in which these techniques can be overlooked if they are seen only as part of evaluation for psychodynamic psychotherapy.

Psychodynamic listening puts the psychiatrist in an attitude of curious inquiry, listening to the meanings, metaphors, developmental sequencing, and interpersonal nuances of the patient's story and of the doctor-patient interaction (2, 3). Particular attention is paid to stories, present and past, about 1) feelings and wishes, 2) the management of various feelings through the life cycle (i.e., defense mechanisms and cognitive style) and areas of healthy interaction with the world, 3) self-esteem regulation, and 4) interpersonal relationships. These four areas reflect the four psychodynamic perspectives on psychopathology: drives, ego function, self psychology, and object relationships (Table 3–1).

The psychodynamic evaluation uses the data obtained from questioning and from psychodynamic listening. The evaluation aims to integrate the patient's chief complaint; history of present illness; past history; family history; developmental history, includ-

TABLE 3–1. **Psychodynamic perspectives**

Theory	Focus
Drive theory	Wishes and feelings
Ego function	Defense mechanisms, cognitive style, and areas of health in the personality
Self psychology	Regulation of self-esteem
Object relations	Internalized memories of interpersonal relationships

ing any traumatic events or deviations from usual developmental patterns; mental status examination; style of doctor-patient interaction; transference; and the psychiatrist's countertransference feelings. The outcome of this evaluation is a psychodynamic understanding of the patient's past and present experiences from the patient's subjective viewpoint. This psychodynamic formulation (4) provides an integrated understanding through the patient's life cycle from the four psychodynamic perspectives on the past and present experiences of the patient, and it makes predictions of potential doctor-patient interactions and the patient's patterns of defense mechanisms and interpersonal interactions.

In this way, the evaluation phase provides information for the assessment of the type and degree of psychiatric illness and impairment, the selection of treatment modality, and the conduct of psychotherapy itself. It is very important before beginning any treatment, particularly psychotherapy, to know the patient's risk of significant depression or mania and to be aware of past suicide attempts by the patient. Without this information, it is extremely difficult to assess the patient's middle-of-the-night call or canceled appointment during a difficult period of the treatment. In addition, the evaluation sets a tone for the psychotherapy. After a well-conducted evaluation, the patient feels respected and safe, believes that his or her best interests are the primary concern of the clinician, and feels that any topic can be talked about.

The therapist's asking about medical signs and symptoms and suicidal and homicidal thoughts and actions frequently relieves the patient of the feeling that he or she is the only one worried about these areas. Often the patient is wondering whether the doctor will ask about these issues. Whether the therapist inquires about these particular areas may be used by the patient as a way to assess whether the therapist is serious about listening and being concerned about the patient or whether these are topics that the clinician feels are irrelevant or too dangerous to talk about. VIP and physician patients in particular are alert to whether the therapist is thorough in the evaluation. The patient who feels that all areas—

medical as well as behavioral—and all risks and concerns have been forthrightly and empathically explored will feel the beginning of a working relationship centered on trust and mutual respect. This beginning is critical to the psychotherapeutic work to follow—work that can include many distortions of the doctor-patient relationship. Commonly, long after a therapy has started—and frequently in its termination phase—a patient may reveal, for example, the one question the therapist asked, or the particular way in which the therapist greeted him or her at the door, that led to the feeling that working together would be possible.

■ BEGINNING THE EVALUATION

The evaluation begins when the therapist meets the patient (5, 6). In the outpatient setting, it is best for the therapist to introduce herself and explain to the patient what the therapist knows about the patient's problems. One should not assume that a patient knows that a session is an evaluation. Rather, the therapist should set the context of the meeting, explaining that she, the therapist, would like to spend some time getting to know the nature of the patient's difficulties and inviting the patient to tell her more (Table 3–2).

The number of evaluation sessions usually ranges from one to four, but more sessions may be needed. The length of the evaluation is determined by the amount of time required to collect the information for the diagnostic and psychodynamic assessment and to address the practical issues of beginning treatment. Usually, the beginning therapist errs on the side of short evaluations and an incomplete assessment. Certainly the evaluation should not extend any longer than necessary. Otherwise, the transference will begin to organize the patient-therapist interaction before the treatment itself has begun. The evaluation sessions are not as well structured as the treatment setting for the emergence and analysis of the transference. If the transference becomes a prominent resistance during the evaluation, it can lead to difficulties in reaching an agreement on the treatment to be pursued. In this case, the transfer-

TABLE 3–2.	**Beginning the evaluation**

Goal

Educate the patient about the evaluation process

Establish an atmosphere of safety and inquiry

Assess for appropriate treatment

Tasks

Assess for life-threatening behaviors

Assess for organic causes of the patient's illness

Determine the diagnosis

Identify areas of conflict across the life cycle

Duration

Meet for one to four sessions

Techniques

Use questioning and listening

Listen for the patient's fears of starting treatment

Attend to the precipitants of the illness and of seeking treatment

---

ence may need to be handled interpretively, and the therapist should be cautious to speak at the level the patient can understand and make use of.

When the clinician is only making the evaluation and the patient will be referred to another therapist for treatment, it is most helpful to the evaluation and to its successful termination that the patient know the plan at the beginning. Then the patient may decide the level of self-disclosure—whether to open up areas that would be too painful to leave unexplored. The therapist must be alert to this issue, because it occurs often in training and clinic settings. Infrequently, it may be advantageous and important to have the initial evaluation done by a clinician who will not be the treating therapist. In the case where the patient needs a very firm, direct, confrontational approach to enter a much-needed treatment, the evaluating clinician who is not expecting to treat the patient may feel freer to be blunt, in a tactful manner, with the patient. The more experienced therapist may be able to be the evaluating clinician and later manage this change in style in an interpretive and psycho-analytic manner, recognizing that an additional parameter has been introduced into the treatment and will require interpretation later on.

The clinician uses two methods for data collection during the evaluation: asking questions and listening unobtrusively (7). Both styles must be used to collect the needed information. A patient complaining of depression should not leave the first evaluation session without the clinician's knowing the severity of the depression and the risk of suicide. This usually requires at least some direct questioning. Life-threatening issues must be dealt with early in order to gather the needed diagnostic information. However, other historical information can be collected as part of the patient's story. Patients must be given the time and space in which to paint a picture of their world without the therapist's choosing the colors! Being either too intrusive or too silent can lead to missed information and can needlessly confuse the patient.

Frequently, the skill of the therapist lies in how the history and diagnostic information are collected. The more skilled the therapist, the more able he or she is to understand—to reach—and therefore to work with a wider range of patients. The skilled therapist can establish a rapport across a wide array of socioeconomic classes and sexual, racial, religious, cultural, and emotional differences. However, all therapists also experience certain therapist-patient differences that they cannot bridge, and in such cases they refer the patient to another clinician.

In the first session the therapist should listen for the patient's fears of starting psychotherapy. These fears should be explored early, as they appear and are articulated by the patient. The patient will feel safer and be more interested in continuing the evaluation and the treatment when these fears have been heard, respected, and explored by the therapist. In addition, airing these fears will leave the therapist in a better position to interpret any precipitous stopping of the treatment. It is not unusual for a patient to drop out during the evaluation phase before beginning treatment. That is one reason to view this phase as the *candidacy* stage. (In clinic settings, about 50% of patients stop before the fifth session.) Early termination may be due to defenses against seeking help, a transference reaction, a decision that this is not the right treatment, or, at times, a relief of symptoms as a result of the evaluation (8).

Usually, by the end of the first session, the clinician will have a plan about how to proceed. What further organic workup is needed? Is psychosis in the differential diagnosis? Are there any life-threatening issues, either now or possibly in the future? At this time, the therapist should explain to the patient approximately how many more sessions will be taken for the evaluation so that the patient has an outline of what is to come.

■ SELECTION CRITERIA

Psychodynamic psychotherapy has its best outcomes with neurotic-level disorders. These disorders have conflicts that are primarily oedipal in nature and that are experienced as internal by the patient. Although the diagnoses in DSM-IV (9) are not organized by their developmental conflict level (or level of maturity of defenses), some of the disorders are more likely than others to present with a primarily neurotic-level conflict. DSM-IV disorders that frequently involve a primarily neurotic conflict include obsessive-compulsive disorder, anxiety disorders, conversion disorder, psychological factors affecting physical disease, dysthymic disorder, mild to moderate mood disorders, adjustment disorders, and mild to moderately severe personality disorders. Patients who are psychologically minded, who are able to observe feelings without acting on them, and who can obtain symptom relief through understanding may benefit from psychodynamic psychotherapy (Table 3–3). The patient who has a supportive environment—family, friends, work—usually does better because he or she is able to use the therapy in a more intensive manner. Such a patient does not need the therapist to be a primary reality support in order to weather the stresses of life or the treatment.

TABLE 3–3.	Patient selection criteria

Patient

    Neurotic-level disorder

    Psychologically minded

    Able to observe feelings without acting on them

    Able to use understanding for relief of symptoms

Environment

    Presence of a supportive environment

Therapist-patient

    Good patient-therapist match

More seriously disturbed patients—those with major depression, schizophrenia, or borderline personality disorder—can also be treated in psychodynamic psychotherapy. For these patients the treatment is usually directed to modifying the illness-onset conditions and facilitating readjustment, recovery, and integration into the community. The regressive tendencies of such patients can be managed in psychodynamic psychotherapy with the use of medication and with greater support and reality feedback through the face-to-face meetings with the therapist. Patients with severe preoedipal pathology are not good candidates for psychodynamic psychotherapy. This type of pathology may be manifested by an inability to form a supportive dyadic relationship, the presence of severely exploitative relationships, a chaotic lifestyle, or substantial (or dangerous) acting out. The basic requirements of psychodynamic psychotherapy—for the patient to have a strong observing ego and an ability to form a supportive therapeutic relationship—are very difficult tasks for these patients.

Although psychology-mindedness is important, intelligence per se is not a selection criterion; in fact, it can reflect a highly organized obsessional character structure that may be very difficult to treat. Socioeconomic class is also not a good predictor of success in treatment. Rather, the ability to work with patients from diverse socioeconomic classes is usually a part of the therapist's task and skill: to span a range of life experiences and accurately empathize with the patient's world. The patient-therapist match, therefore, is very important, especially to the opening phase of treatment and the establishment of the therapeutic alliance. In general, patients who like their therapists, who have had a shorter duration of symptoms, and who are seeking understanding of their problems as well as symptom relief have the best outcomes. The use of a trial interpretation during the evaluation phase can provide much useful information on how the patient makes use of understanding to modify symptoms and to what extent the patient experiences understanding provided through interpretation as supportive and helpful (10).

■ REFERENCES

1. Ursano RJ, Silberman EK: Individual psychotherapies, in The American Psychiatric Press Textbook of Psychiatry. Edited by Talbott JA, Hales RE, Yudofsky SC. Washington, DC, American Psychiatric Press, 1988, pp 855–889
2. Mohl PC, McLaughlin GDW: Listening to the patient, in Psychiatry. Edited by Tasman A, Kaye J, Lieberman J. Philadelphia, PA, WB Saunders, 1996, pp 3–18
3. Edelson M: Telling and enacting stories in psychoanalysis and psychodynamic psychotherapy. Psychoanal Study Child 48:293–325, 1993
4. Perry S, Cooper AM, Michels R: The psychodynamic formulation: its purpose, structure and clinical application. Am J Psychiatry 144:543–550, 1987
5. Lazare A, Eisenthal S: Clinician/patient relations, I: attending to the patient's perspective, in Outpatient Psychiatry. Edited by Lazare A. Baltimore, MD, Williams & Wilkins, 1989, pp 125–136
6. Lazare A, Eisenthal S, Frank A: Clinician/patient relations, II: conflict and negotiation, in Outpatient Psychiatry. Edited by Lazare A. Baltimore, MD, Williams & Wilkins, 1989, pp 137–157
7. Silberman EK, Certa K: Psychiatric interview: settings and techniques, in Psychiatry. Edited by Tasman A, Kaye J, Lieberman J. Philadelphia, PA, WB Saunders, 1996, pp 19–39

8. Malan DH, Heath ES, Baral HA, et al: Psychodynamic changes in untreated neurotic patients, II: apparently genuine improvement. Arch Gen Psychiatry 32:110–126, 1973

9. American Psychiatric Association: Diagnostic and Statistical Manual of Mental Disorders, 4th Edition. Washington, DC, American Psychiatric Association, 1994

10. Malan DH: Toward the Validation of Dynamic Psychotherapy. New York, Plenum, 1980

■ ADDITIONAL READINGS

Brook HE: Empathy: misconceptions and misuses in psychotherapy. Am J Psychiatry 145:420–424, 1988

Levinson D, Merrifield J, Berg K: Becoming a patient. Arch Gen Psychiatry 17:385–406, 1967

Malan DH: Individual Psychotherapy and the Science of Psychodynamics. London, Butterworths, 1979

Strupp HH, Hadley SW: Negative effects and their determinants, in Negative Outcome in Psychotherapy and What to Do About It. Edited by Mays DT, Franks CM. New York, Springer, 1985, pp 20–55

Bergen AE, Garfield, SL (eds): Handbook of Psychotherapy and Behavior Change. New York, Wiley, 1994

4

PATIENT EVALUATION, II: PSYCHODYNAMIC LISTENING

Listening to patients psychodynamically, a centerpiece of psycho-dynamic psychotherapy, has many applications. Such listening is required when doing an evaluation for psychodynamic psychotherapy or supportive psychotherapy and to develop a psychodynamic evaluation to aid medication compliance. Such listening is also useful in consultation-liaison evaluations, in inpatient assessments, and in evaluations aimed primarily at finding the right form of medication for a psychiatric patient.

What is psychodynamic listening? The answer is not simple, and experienced teachers of psychoanalysis and psychodynamic psychotherapy might emphasize different components. The view presented here is an attempt to integrate various schools of thought—an attempt that borrows from dominant contemporary theoretical positions about the nature of the human mind and about how to listen for evidence of health and malfunction from these viewpoints.

■ THE FOUR PSYCHOLOGIES

Today, four major psychological perspectives are employed in the psychodynamic understanding of mental function (1–4). These are drive theory, ego psychology, self psychology, and object relations theory (Table 4–1).

According to drive theory, certain inborn, biologically based instincts are responsible for different wishes during different

TABLE 4–1. **The four psychodynamic psychologies of mental function**

Psychology	Prominent concepts
Drive theory	Biologically based instincts prominent (libido/aggression)
	Modern perspective: wishes
	Sexual (bodily) development important determinant of conflict areas
Ego psychology	Adaptation and regulation of drives prominent
	Defense mechanisms
	Nonconflicted areas of mental function are resources (intelligence, perception, memory, etc.)
Self psychology	Regulation of self-esteem and self-worth
	Early parent-child relationships important
	Separation/individuation important developmental task
Object relations theory	Memories of important figures from the past organize wishes, behavior, perception, and meaning
	Development takes place in the context of relationships

phases of human development. For example, in the view of a drive theorist, the wish of an adolescent boy to find a girlfriend and pair off with her, and then to experiment sexually with her, reflects an instinctually based process. Although today many drive theorists no longer take literally the idea of instincts and drives, the metaphorical notion of a libidinal drive—a drive that includes wishes involving feelings of love and sexual desire—is seen as a central motivating force in human thinking, feeling, and behaving.

The second psychodynamic perspective is ego psychology. In this theory of mental function, the mind grows to have psychological capabilities that include abilities to regulate and control the drives. Sometimes this process of regulation involves keeping wishes outside conscious awareness through the use of defense mechanisms, described elsewhere in this book (see Chapter 7). Sometimes control involves an awareness of one's wishes and of the activities and thoughts designed to make them happen. Thus, the ego psychologist studies the way a person thinks, cognitive styles, defense mechanisms, activity designed to actualize or block the fulfillment of a wish, and nonconflicted areas of mental function that can provide resources and strengths for development (e.g., intelligence, perception, memory).

Self psychology, the third psychodynamic perspective on mental function, emphasizes that to understand a person, it is essential to study the way she or he has developed self-esteem and now regulates self-esteem. This line of psychological development focuses on the early parent-child relationship—specifically, the ways parents convey to very young children a sense of themselves, their separateness, and their worth. In later life the ability to function effectively as a separate person, with a sense of self-worth that withstands the normal disappointments of life, reflects a healthy experience in this developmental realm.

Object relations theory, the fourth psychodynamic theory, focuses on the organized sets of memories of important figures from the past and of oneself—the pictures of individuals inside one's mind, including the self and those others who have been important figures in one's life. These individuals might include members of the family of origin, close friends, spouses, children, and teachers, as well as many others. All that is required is that these people have been important to the person and that organized sets of memories of each exist within the person's mind. According to object relations theory, individuals cannot effectively be studied from the perspective of drive, defense (ego psychology), and self-esteem without recognizing that human development takes place in a context of relationships. These relationships create the memories described above, and these memories of relationships motivate the individual to wish for certain gratifications and to attempt to satisfy those wishes in certain ways, all within the context of relationships with others.

Several additional theoretical positions grow out of these dominant four. The intersubjective perspective holds that each person's truth is highly personal and unique—that there is no such thing as objectivity or objective truth when studying a person. The therapeutic relationship is, therefore, an exercise in intersubjective interaction and mutual assessment, in which the therapist perceives and considers only his or her own version of what is going on. The interpersonal perspective focuses on the relationship of the therapist and patient, studying that interaction while placing relatively less emphasis on the patient's past. Other perspectives focus on motivational theory in ways that depart from the more traditional theories of drives, self, and interpersonal relations.

■ THE CLINICAL MOMENT AND CLINICAL ASSESSMENT

What this very brief summary attempts to convey is the framework in which the psychodynamic therapist listens to clinical data (1–4). As the psychiatrist listens to the patient speak, in consultation or in ongoing therapy, he or she experiences, in his or her own mind, clinical moments, in which the state of the patient's mind is examined in detail from the perspectives of the four psychologies (Table 4–2).

The clinician listener wonders, "What is this person wishing for, and how does that reflect the development of his basic wishes—the nature of his basic wishes?" (drive theory)

The clinician asks herself, "What happens to those wishes? Are they kept unconscious by the defenses, or are they admitted into consciousness? If they are conscious, does the individual move effectively toward actualizing them? Or are there ways in which the individual prevents them from being actualized, a second layer of defenses?" (ego psychology)

The clinician further ponders, "How does this person feel about

TABLE 4–2. Psychodynamic listening from the perspective of the four psychologies of mental function

Psychology	Considerations
Drive theory	What is the patient wishing for?
	What in the patient's history caused this wish to be prominent?
	Are the wishes developmentally appropriate?
Ego psychology	What events in the history of the patient indicate the expression or inhibition of wishes?
	How does the patient keep wishes out of conscious awareness? (defenses)
Self psychology	Does the patient like her/himself?
	Does she/he feel valued, admired, recognized by others?
	How does he/she respond to events that decrease self-esteem or remove admiring or valuing others from his/her life?
Object relations theory	Who are the prominent people in the patient's past and present?
	How are these people recalled at the different stages of development?
	Who from the past does the patient behave, feel, and think like?
	Who does the patient miss and long for?
	Who was lost from the patient's life at an early age? (Lost by death or moving or loss due to illness or conflict)

himself right now? Does he like himself, and if not, will he be able to tolerate that and to figure out how to arrange his life so that soon he will like himself again? Does he have a capacity to regulate his self-esteem on his own, or does he have to use others, sometimes in ways that reflect a lack of feeling for them, to make himself feel better?"(self psychology)

Finally, the clinician thinks, "Who are the important people within this person's mind? How does he remember them and use them—as models for his own thinking and behavior, or as models for his own wishes and for the people he seeks out? Does he seek them out directly?" (object relations theory)

The clinician using psychodynamic listening, mindful of the ephemeral nature of truth, tries to place herself in the position of the patient and see the world through that person's eyes. The psychodynamic listener knows that her relationship with her patient is an interpersonal relationship. She wonders about what that relationship is revealing about the patient's ways of thinking, feeling, and living and also about what from the patient's past is being transferred into that shared relationship.

Yet there is more to how the psychodynamic listener functions, at least within the psychotherapeutic situation. In an evaluation, the assessment of many clinical moments, coupled with the more usual taking of a history, may be enough to reach a clinical conclusion and make a recommendation. In ongoing psychodynamic therapy, the therapist experiences clinical moment after clinical moment, all this taking place within a special context. For in psychodynamic psychotherapy the therapist is pulled by the patient into that patient's world—or at least, a simulated microcosm of that world within the four walls of the therapy consulting room. There the psychodynamically listening psychotherapist uses her capacity to observe and assess clinical moments to place into perspective what is going on in this experience. It is an intense experience involving two people who share a healing task, even as they share a situation in which each experiences transference feelings toward the other because both regress under the pressure of the therapeutic situation (5–7).

In this chapter we discuss an example of psychodynamic listening in a consultation-liaison situation, followed by discussion of an example of how such listening was central in evaluation for psychotherapy. Then we add further discussion of the psychodynamic psychotherapy situation, including an elaboration of

- How the patient's world is recreated,
- How the therapist is drawn into it,
- How transference and countertransference develop and are experienced, and
- How psychodynamic listening is used by the therapist to derive an understanding of the patient, develop a strategy of how to help the patient, and arrive at tactical interventions to promote a healing process.

■ PSYCHODYNAMIC LISTENING IN A CONSULTATION-LIAISON SITUATION

A psychiatrist was called upon to evaluate an outpatient who complained of intractable pain. The patient, in her forties, was a professional woman and a wife and mother who had had lower-back surgery 2 years earlier. Although the surgery had been successful, as far as follow-up X-ray and magnetic resonance imaging (MRI) studies revealed, and although the neurological examination revealed no hard neurological signs, she complained of sharp pains in the area of her surgery, sometimes radiating down her legs.

The consulting psychiatrist explained at their first meeting that the entire medical team knew that this woman was experiencing significant pain, that there was no suggestion that her discomfort was imaginary. He added that sometimes processes within the mind could produce or contribute to bodily reactions of pleasure, and sometimes of pain, and that by talking about her life, her hopes, her wishes, her frustrations—both past and present—and her expectations for her future, he might be able to help her obtain some measure of relief.

It must be stressed that this patient was a very bright and sophisticated person and that this approach by the

consulting psychiatrist was appreciated by her. Yet she
was doubtful that he would come up with anything. In
any event, she agreed to meet with him, and they went on
from there. She revealed that she was the oldest of four
children, born in a rural setting on a family farm. Her two
younger brothers still worked the farm, her parents having recently retired. She recounted that early in life she
had demonstrated academic gifts and had received special encouragement from her parents and teachers. From
her early teens on she was sent to special enrichment
programs in the summer: first at the local college, then at
the major research state university of her home state, and
eventually at a very prestigious private university in a
major metropolitan area in the region in which her family
lived. There she met other bright young people from all
parts of the United States. She and other students in
attendance collectively dreamed about attending college
there together. While all this was happening, her brothers, sister, and parents worked the family farm through
summers when there were too much rain, too much sun,
crop diseases, and other conditions making financial
survival difficult.

The psychiatrist was already wondering, during this
first consultation session, about what this woman was
trying to tell him. He wondered, "Why has she chosen to
tell me about herself and her family in just this way, at
the start?" He found himself picturing this woman living
in a state of relative luxury while the rest of her family
toiled. But why would she emphasize this, especially
when she was in so much pain?

In their second 45-minute meeting this patient chose
to talk about her current life. She was a lawyer, working
for a large corporation. The work was hard and the
standards demanding. She had two children, both young
teenagers, both academically gifted. She felt close to

both of them and proud of both of them. She had been married for 20 years to a man she loved. She said they had met when she was in law school. He was a partner in a law firm in the city in which they lived. Then she spoke of a vacation trip they had taken a couple of years earlier, back to the family farm. It had been in the summer, and she, her husband, and their two children had spent 2 weeks on the farm. She noted that she had wanted to take this kind of a vacation—that she had felt an increasing distance from her family and had planned it as a way of getting closer.

It was nearing the end of the time allotted for this second session, and the psychiatrist had already begun to consider what he had learned. In constructing in his own mind several clinical moments, he knew much about his patient's handling of her wishes, the defenses and personality characteristics she used in relation to these wishes, her sense of herself, and the ways in which she related to the people in her object world. She was a woman who could define what she wanted: academic success, professional success, a loving and sexual relationship with her husband, an encouraging and close relationship with her children. Her defenses and character style were productive: rather than repress her aggressive wishes for success—for what she wanted—she had a capacity to articulate her desires and channel her energies into constructive activities allowing her to obtain them. This represented a well refined capacity to sublimate. He speculated that she employed a certain amount of defensive altruism and that perhaps that motivated the trip back to the farm, but he was impressed that this was a person who was capable of defining and reaching her goals. Her good capacity to regulate her self-esteem was clear, and she possessed a rich world of relationships and mental representations of the people she had known. In sum, she was well put together.

At that moment the patient began to talk about how her back trouble started. When on the farm, she decided that she should pitch in on the chores that her brothers, their wives, and her nieces and nephews shared, and in doing farm chores she had injured her back. Yet at the time she felt compelled to keep working, and in doing so she aggravated an injury that might otherwise have healed. In closing this session, the psychiatrist asked his patient why, immediately after her injury, she hadn't stopped doing the work she was obviously not used to. She responded without missing a beat that throughout her life her parents and siblings had worked hard and that she had derived much personal benefit as the result of their efforts. She simply could not have stopped helping during the visit.

The psychiatrist now believed that he had not only obtained needed historical data, but that from the perspective of ego psychology he had learned a great deal. He now knew that although this woman was not guilt-ridden in a pathological sense, she had a demanding conscience and a defensive structure that reflected that: the altruism about which he had previously speculated had been confirmed. To her, success was not performing farm chores, but her ego demanded that she do them while visiting her family.

In the next session the psychiatrist decided to ask his patient about the details of the history of her surgery, her rehabilitation, and the nature of her current life and her back pain. She was very forthcoming, yet she revealed another aspect of her defensive structure: she was not particularly introspective. She revealed that she had returned home from her vacation in pain and that she had done nothing about it because there was a very demanding legal case at her corporation to which she had to devote a great deal of time. Then, as she discussed her work in more detail, she described it as "backbreaking." She reported that whenever a case heated up, she worked extremely long hours at her desk, often depriving herself of sleep and often feeling physically ill. At such times her neck and back would always ache. As she said this, she made no connection to her current situation, but the psychiatrist wondered about a relationship.

She went on to describe how her back pain had become unbearable, how efforts at rehabilitation had failed, and how eventually she had had surgery. The psychiatrist asked her whether during this preoperative period she had tried to spend less time at her desk. She said she had not been able to do that, that it had been a busy time, adding "I was raised to work hard. I had a good mind, and I escaped the farm, but I was taught to work hard anyway."

The psychiatrist now offered some of his observations to his patient. He noted that she had been hurt trying to work side by side with members of her family who were used to working with their bodies. She had felt she could not quit, even when she was in pain. When she returned home, she continued to work—at a job that she thought of as "backbreaking" and that in fact often caused her to feel pain in her neck and back. He pointed out that she was very appreciative of what had been done for her by her family and felt an obligation to be loyal, to be hard-working, and even to "break her back" to serve those who employed her or those who helped her. She agreed with all these observations, but in keeping with her style of minimal introspection, she could think of nothing to add. Therefore the psychiatrist wondered whether she was taking care of her back now or continuing to work at her "backbreaking" job as she had before. He noted: "Perhaps you are in so much pain because your conscience tells you that you must work, and you sit at your desk for hours on end, bringing on much of the pain because you are doing something physically that would cause anyone pain. Has anyone told you that sitting is very hard on the back—that it can cause intense back and neck pain?"

At that point, this very bright woman acknowledged that she had never known this fact. Although, to her psychiatrist, this suggested that perhaps she had not received adequate postoperative rehabilitative care, he also speculated that she had been so driven by her need to work side by side with her brothers and parents, literally and metaphorically, at her legal job that she had been unable to hear what had been advised by her physical therapist and her surgeon. He confirmed this by consulting with her physical therapist. At that point, the psychiatrist set about educating his patient about the strength of her conscience and the rigid way it directed her and prevented her from changing her lifestyle enough that she could get over her back pain. That meant taking time out to exercise and spending fewer hours at her desk.

More physical therapy followed, and in time this patient got over the intense pain of muscle spasms, which were actually treatable with exercise and judicious judgment about how to structure her work life. Eventually, she was even able to work almost as hard as she had before, taking breaks at intervals to stretch. Common sense (which she had always possessed) was now more effective in keeping her pain free, even during times of intense legal work, because a carefully listening, psychodynamically oriented consultant had spent several hours talking with this basically industrious, successful, loving woman. Although she did not become basically different—not suddenly introspective—she did now understand a psychodynamic set of factors that had previously prevented her from taking care of herself. She could now avoid the "backbreaking" pain she had unconsciously felt she owed her family of origin, whose hard physical labor had paved the way for her to enjoy a life filled with luxuries they could only imagine.

■ PSYCHODYNAMIC LISTENING IN A PSYCHOTHERAPY EVALUATION

A patient was referred to a senior psychiatrist by a less experienced colleague, who had done an initial evaluation and believed psychotherapy was in order. Yet the younger colleague, who practiced general psychiatry and was unsure of exactly what kind of therapy to recommend, asked the older psychiatrist to complete the evaluation and undertake the treatment. The patient was a single man in his early thirties, well educated and actively working at his career. He had a girlfriend, and he stated that he was doing well at work, had many colleagues with whom he was on good terms, and had many friends, male and female. He indicated that he came from a happy family, was the middle of three brothers with whom he got on well, and was close to both his parents. He described a happy childhood, again with many friends. Academics had been easy for him, although he had not been a particularly good student, and because he was so affable he had many offers for jobs in the business world upon college graduation.

Similarly, the man reported that for his entire life he had gotten along well with women. He recalled his first girlfriend in fourth grade, an active dating life in high school and thereafter, sexual experimentation beginning in adolescence, and a sex life he had enjoyed since his college days. Everything had been going well until anxiety attacks had begun about a year earlier. A careful history revealed that for several months before he experienced the frank outbreak of anxiety, he had been sleeping poorly—for reasons he could not explain. Then, one day while in his car in a traffic jam, he noticed that he began to breath heavily, perspire, experience a rapid heartbeat, and feel frightened. He went to his doctor, an internist, who found nothing during a complete examination. The man was told that he had experienced an anxiety or panic attack. This doctor asked him whether there was something on his mind, and he responded that there was not. The doctor told him that this phenomenon might have been an isolated one, but that if it happened again, he should return for medication.

When the patient experienced a second episode a month later, he called his doctor and was given a prescription for a benzodiazepine, to be taken as needed. Several more attacks occurred over the next several months, and he was referred by his internist for evaluation by the general psychiatrist. That physician was impressed by the careful way the patient presented his history and noted that the patient was articulate. When the patient complained about being drowsy when he used the medication even occasionally, the psychiatrist thought that a form of talking therapy might be the proper treatment. The patient went on to report that he was quite sensitive to any medication with any sedating properties and that for that reason he also abstained from alcohol. When the referral for psychotherapy evaluation was made, the general psychiatrist believed the patient was an ideal candidate for psychodynamic psychotherapy.

The senior psychiatrist, for her part, was not so sure. She was struck at the outset that the patient was not at all introspective, reporting a picture-perfect previous life that sounded too good to be true; and, in her opinion, drowsiness was an indication for further medication adjustment, not psychodynamic psychotherapy. But she proceeded to take a history, listening from the perspective of the four psychologies.

She heard the patient clearly expressing his wishes for success in business and in his social life. When she asked about his 3-year relationship with his girlfriend, he said that she was fun and pretty and that he enjoyed participation with her in sex, sports, and a summer beach house they shared with several other young men and women. Although the psychiatrist devoted an entire 45-minute session to discussing this relationship, nothing more emerged. The psychiatrist was therefore impressed that in the view of this man, the relationship involved no commitment—no sense of long-term connection or responsibility. She also hypothesized that this man maintained distance in this potentially intimate relationship as a defense against recognizing that he was not a boy, but a man; and she believed that he had no appreciation at all of this defense or its purpose. Therefore, from the perspective of drive theory and ego psychology, the psychiatrist concluded that there was in this man much defensive activity directed against recognizing the meaning of his wishes: there was conflict within him about seeing himself as, and wishing to be, a strong, capable, responsible, sexual man. He was happier thinking of himself as a person still in late adolescence, and he was unaware of any of these mental positions, preferences, or processes.

The psychiatrist wondered about the cause of such conflict, but when she probed this man's life as a child and his relationships to those in his family of origin, no readily available information was forthcoming. Nor was there an indication of difficulty in the area of self-esteem regulation, which might have further explained the clinical picture. The psychiatrist knew, of course, that those who had problems with the development of the self and with the maintenance of self-esteem often lacked a capacity to see others as whole people with feelings and needs of their own; and she knew that their relationships were often designed to maintain self-esteem by providing rather superficial gratification of their needs. But there was no clear history of a problem in this area, despite the history of the patient's relationship with his girlfriend. The psychiatrist therefore concluded that from the perspective of self psychology all might not be well, but that nothing definitive could be said. From the perspective of the patient's object world, also, all might not be well, but a definitive conclusion could not be reached. Certainly the patient described elaborate internal pictures of many people; and although there was a certain hard-to-define lack of depth to these descriptions, nothing specific could be said about an inhibiting oedipal constellation or a defect in the capacity to form and maintain relationships.

The evaluating psychiatrist in a situation like this cannot conclude that in-depth talking therapy will not someday be indicated or that it will not be helpful in the future. However, a recommendation for probing psychodynamic psychotherapy would be inappropriate in this kind of patient because of his symptom-focused chief complaint, the absence of a history of long-standing and complex psychological pain, a presentation of a rather superficial, uninvolved personality style, and a marked lack of introspection and motivation for a detailed process of looking inward. The most prudent approach seemed to be a recommendation for supportive psychotherapy, conducted concurrently with medication management, by a psychiatrist well trained in psychodynamically based supportive psychotherapy and able to respond if this patient later wanted to examine his problems more closely.

The patient was referred again to the general psychiatrist with the recommendation that every other week a full 45-minute psychotherapy session be held, during which medication would be discussed, along with the feelings the patient had about his condition and his life. The further recommendation, that the general psychiatrist consult every month or two with the senior psychiatrist, to reconsider the possibility that the patient's complaint about medication was an indication of a wish for more deeply probing talking therapy, was also well received. The patient then began regular visits with the general psychiatrist, who did consult regularly.

■ PSYCHODYNAMIC LISTENING IN THE CONTEXT OF PSYCHODYNAMIC PSYCHOTHERAPY

A single man in his late thirties was referred for in-depth psychodynamic psychotherapy by a psychiatrist skilled in psychodynamic psychotherapy. The patient was a well-educated teacher who had never been married; he reported that he was adopted and that his adoptive father had abandoned the family when the patient was 7 years old. He noted that his adoptive mother had tried to meet his needs and to raise him well but had failed because of her own sense of inadequacy, her own lack of clear ideas about what to teach him, her own dependency on him, and her own tendency to be smothering. He reported that he was chronically unhappy, dissatisfied with his accomplishments, and unable to form lasting relationships.

This was especially disturbing to him in respect to women. He felt very lonely and longed for romance.

After several evaluation sessions the psychiatrist concluded that this introspective, chronically unhappy man had problems in many spheres. His capacity to define his wishes was substantially impaired, and, along with inhibitions, he was employing many defenses against an awareness of his aggressive capacities. The psychiatrist hypothesized that this personality style was the result of powerful though unconscious aggressive wishes directed at his imagined biological parents, who had abandoned him; his abandoning adoptive father; and his inept adoptive mother. The psychiatrist also concluded that because of so many abandonments and such failed parenting, this man constantly feared personal rejection and therefore maintained his distance in all relationships. This was reflected in the details of his descriptions of memories of the individuals with whom he had related over the years. There had never been close friendships, romances, or even close relationships with those with whom he worked. His sense of himself was fragile, and he anticipated professional failure and rejection constantly despite the consistent academic success that had resulted in his career as a teacher. Indeed, although he felt very disconnected from people, there was evidence that his professional colleagues prized their opportunities to interact with him.

The psychiatrist was impressed that two great strengths possessed by this man were his intellect and his capacity for introspection, and that those strengths, combined with his being in deep psychological pain and sincerely wanting help, meant that psychodynamic psychotherapy should be tried. The psychiatrist was aware that this man's liabilities would characterize the transference in that therapy: he expected the patient to be distant and distrustful and eventually to want to leave the treatment when their relationship threatened to become close. The psychiatrist was also aware that the reasons for this man's strengths were unclear: why was he so intellectual and introspective? It would have been helpful to be able to answer that question at the start, for with that insight might have come an enhanced capacity to formulate a prognosis. But, despite all that was unknown, the patient's strengths were evident. The treatment was recommended to him, and he agreed to begin.

Almost at once the treatment foundered. The patient complained bitterly that the psychiatrist was not helping him enough. The patient developed psychosomatic complaints: abdominal pain, headaches, and backaches, none of which were helped by the talking therapy sessions, which lasted 50 minutes and were held three times each week. The patient soon stated that he was going to "quit this worthless therapy." The psychiatrist, for his part, dreaded each session. He found himself wishing that his patient would not show up, that the patient would quit. But, because he was a well-trained psychodynamic therapist, he knew that he should regard this intense, mutual early experience of therapy as the result of the patient's effort to recreate his psychological world in the consulting room and to convey something of that world to his psychotherapist. He knew that what the patient felt toward him should be examined from the perspective of transference and that his feelings toward his patient should be viewed as an example of countertransference, thought of as a set of feelings that would inform him about the patient's life experience. (See Chapters 8 and 9 in this volume.)

Because the psychiatrist knew that the patient had created in their relationship a version of his world, he also knew that to help this therapy along he had to explain to the patient something of what might be going on (5–7). The psychiatrist knew that an assertion by him that he knew exactly what was happening would be seen as ludicrous by this carefully thinking patient, but the psychiatrist hoped that an honest effort at an approximation would not be. So he explained to the patient that he had been abandoned and disappointed so many times, and at such a young age, that he was profoundly afraid to relate to others with trust and with the hope that they would remain loyal to him and available when he needed them. The therapist also explained that, because these experiences had occurred at a time when his language development was immature, he often expressed himself with his body. That was why so many of his complaints had been psychosomatic and also why he felt so profoundly disappointed when the talking therapy had not immediately worked to relieve these symptoms. The patient experienced the therapeutic relationship as he had experienced relationships he had had as a very young child who had already been abandoned: indeed, he had already abandoned hope of the therapy!

The psychiatrist went on to note that this man was very well motivated for treatment and that he might view his early presentation of himself—his construction of his world within the consulting room—as a creative, unconsciously motivated effort to convey to his psychotherapist what his world had been, and was, all about. The psychiatrist suggested that the patient had transferred onto the psychiatrist his fears of abandonment and his certainty that he would not be helped when he needed it. The psychiatrist said further that the patient had tried, through the way he treated his psychiatrist, to create in his psychiatrist a sense of hopelessness to convey to him how hopeless he, the patient, felt.

The psychiatrist went on to say that the patient had

developed these feelings quickly and forcefully because he was so afraid of disappointment. It was important, the psychiatrist continued, that the two of them have a meeting of the minds to develop a way to handle such an intense relationship so that it could be useful to the patient. The psychiatrist also explained to his patient his view of what transference was: unconsciously motivated ways all people have of orienting themselves in the world, framing current experience in terms of remembered or repressed past experience.

All this made sense to the patient, reinforcing in the psychiatrist the opinion that they were on the right track. The psychiatrist recognized that through psychodynamic listening in the therapy he had been able to develop hypotheses about the patient's wishes, fears, and defenses within their relationship and about the representation of himself as a transference figure within his patient's mind. He had known, too, that the fragile state of his patient's sense of self had made it imperative that a quick response from the psychiatrist be forthcoming, lest the patient bolt the therapy as his pain became unbearable. Finally, he knew that he and his patient needed to keep in mind the importance of speaking about such states of mind as the patient experienced them. This practice would reinforce the reality that their relationship would endure and that the patient would not be abandoned. The strategy that had evolved was to explore the patient's experience of his therapist as a potentially abandoning figure. From a tactical perspective, the decision had been made to do this rapidly—not to let such fears build, as might be done with a patient who had greater confidence in others. The psychiatrist knew that the best form of reassurance for this man, within the context of psychodynamic psychotherapy, was to aggressively anticipate and to examine his patient's experience of how fragile their relationship was.

This therapy continued for 4 years; and as the patient improved and his understanding of himself grew, he was able to tolerate longer and longer periods of his intense transference fear of abandonment. At the end of his successful treatment, he was able to remind himself when necessary of how powerful was the effect of his disappointing early life. At that point, he was engaged to be married and had developed the capacity for closeness with friends and colleagues. Additionally, he had developed the ability to tolerate separations and disagreements with those with whom he had become close, including his future wife, without falling apart: his capacity to experience his fears and maintain his perspective that life would go on was greatly enhanced. Further, he did not usually experience fear of abandonment with what he now saw as the irrational intensity that had characterized his life experience before psychodynamic treatment.

That a crucial component of his newly developed equilibrium was his ability to reassure himself illustrates an important truth about psychodynamic psychotherapy. It does not work by magic. In large measure, it works because the patient learns within the psychotherapeutic situation to listen to himself psychodynamically, to think about himself more completely, to assess with more perspective what he is experiencing, and to provide for himself the explanations of his experience that are needed in order to maintain a state of psychological balance.

■ REFERENCES

1. Chessick RD: The Technique and Practice of Listening in Intensive Psychotherapy. Northvale, NJ, Jason Aronson, 1989
2. Detrick DW, Detrick SP: Self Psychology: Comparisons and Contrasts. Hillsdale, NJ, Analytic Press, 1989

3. Pine F: The four psychologies of psychoanalysis and their place in clinical work. J Am Psychoanal Assoc 36:571–596, 1988
4. Pulver SE: The eclectic analyst, or the many roads to insight and change. J Am Psychoanal Assoc 41:339–357, 1993
5. Gardner MR: Self Inquiry. Hillsdale, NJ, Analytic Press, 1989
6. Jacobs TJ: The Use of the Self: Countertransference and Communication in the Analytic Situation. Madison, CT, International Universities Press, 1991
7. Sonnenberg SM: The analyst's self-analysis and its impact on clinical work: a comment on the sources and importance of personal insights. J Am Psychoanal Assoc 39:687–704, 1991

■ ADDITIONAL READINGS

McLaughlin JT: Work with patients and the experience of self-analysis, in Self-Analysis: Critical Inquiries, Personal Visions. Edited by Barron JW. Hillsdale, NJ, Analytic Press, 1993, pp 63–81
Smith HF: Engagements in analysis and their use in self-analysis, in Self-Analysis: Critical Inquiries, Personal Visions. Edited by Barron JW. Hillsdale, NJ, Analytic Press, 1993, pp 83–110

5

PATIENT EVALUATION, III:
PSYCHODYNAMIC
EVALUATION

A psychodynamic evaluation uses both inquiry and psychodynamic listening to develop an integrated understanding of the patient's chief complaint, the history of present illness, the past medical and psychiatric history, and the family history. It includes the following components:

- The performance of a mental status examination
- The construction of a developmental psychological history of significant life events
- An evaluation of the role of trauma and developmental deficits in shaping the individual's psychological makeup
- The articulation of a prognosis reflecting different treatment options
- A prediction of the nature of the doctor-patient interaction in individual psychodynamic psychotherapy; the assessment of the doctor-patient interaction takes into account 1) the assets and liabilities of the patient and how they will influence the transference-countertransference situation and 2) the ability of the doctor-patient dyad to use this interaction therapeutically
- An assessment of the patient's ability to observe the workings of his own mind and the implications of his behavior, which is especially important

The evaluation examines the metaphors and symbols the patient uses, both consciously and unconsciously, and the patient's ability to understand that what he says may be understood on multiple levels by exploring these symbols. Similarly, the patient's dreams may be considered, as well as his ability to think about dreams as a vehicle for understanding how his mind works. Patterns in the patient's life history are considered, both from the perspective of self-destructive tendencies that might limit the ability to undertake a psychodynamic psychotherapy and from the perspective of the ability to delay gratification and deal with aggressive feelings constructively. Childhood experiences are brought into focus, and the patient's capacity to adapt is traced from that time to the present. Early memories are explored, as are the capacities to function in an autonomous fashion and to work toward the actualization of goals and desires.

The outcome of this evaluation is a psychodynamic understanding of the patient's past and present experiences from the patient's subjective viewpoint. This psychodynamic formulation (1, 2) provides an integrated understanding, across the patient's life cycle, of the past and present experiences of the patient from the four psychodynamic perspectives (feelings, wishes; defense mechanisms, cognitive style; self-esteem regulation; interpersonal relationships). The formulation also makes predictions of potential doctor-patient interactions and the patient's patterns of defense mechanisms and interpersonal interactions.

The data of the psychodynamic evaluation are the patient's history and interaction with the clinician (3). The precipitant of the patient's problems and the precipitant for seeking help provide a particularly helpful window on the active unconscious conflicts, the patterned problems of childhood that are unresolved and still affecting adult behavior (Table 5–1). Detailed exploration of the conditions of the onset of the illness is very important to understanding the psychodynamics of the patient's problem. For example, one patient presented with anxiety symptoms manifest as chest pain. The pains began shortly after he witnessed a man at a movie theater having a heart attack. Another patient had the onset of depressive symptoms shortly after being selected for a promotion. The pattern of the onset conditions provides the outline of the underlying unconscious conflict to be discovered.

The manner in which the patient relates to the clinician also provides information on how interpersonal relations are patterned and on potential transference responses. One male patient seeing a male therapist was very careful not to offend, asking the clinician which of the two offered hours for a return visit would be better for him. In another case a female patient with a female therapist asked casually, as she left the office, where the therapist had gotten her shoes, adding, "But they would be too expensive for me." Although not all the meanings of these interactions are clear initially, the clinician should note them. Such interactions provide additional data that must fit the hypothesized formulation of the patient's character style and conflict areas. The beginning therapist may jump to explore these interactions. However, drawing the patient's attention to these comments early in the therapy relationship is usually frightening for the patient and results in stifling the patient's curiosity and emerging transference. The therapist fre-

---

TABLE 5–1. **Psychodynamic assessment guidelines**

Listen to and explore precipitants of illness and of seeking help.

Listen to and explore history of significant events and people from childhood to the present.

Identify the significant figures in the past.

Ask for the earliest memory.

Explore any recurrent or recent dream and the context of when it was dreamed.

Discuss the patient's experience of previous treatments and therapists.

Observe how the patient relates to the therapist.

Give a trial interpretation.

Invite collaboration in understanding.

---

quently does not have to respond at all, but rather can listen or rephrase a question (e.g., "Whichever session you prefer"). The interactions will recur at a later date, when they can be more fully explored.

The patient's history provides the template for the patterning of the present relationships and defensive styles (4, 5). The psychodynamic therapist listens to the patient's history for the conflicts that were experienced throughout development and for the significant figures with whom the conflicts were experienced: mother, father, grandparent, sister, brother. These conflicts hold the potentials for the transference that will emerge in treatment when the past is alive in the present. The clinician collects a detailed description of each family member—the players in the drama of the patient's life—and of how they were experienced (6).

It is important to remember that the father of the 5-year-old is not necessarily the father of the 15-year-old. Parents change as events happen in their own lives: the birth of additional children, job changes, the death of their own parents. The father who was seen as overdomineering at one age may have been helpful in structuring at another. History should be collected for each of the important periods of the patient's life—for example, preschool, elementary school, high school, early employment or college, and marriage. Understanding how the patient experienced each of these periods of time, who the important people were at that time, and what significant events occurred can identify early patterns of feelings and relationships that are now problematic in the patient's life.

Asking the patient his or her earliest memory frequently reveals an important recurrent theme in the patient's life; it can also be used to assess the patient's willingness and ability to explore fantasy material. Similarly, asking the patient to report a recent or recurrent dream and briefly exploring it with the patient provides content for the formulation of conflict areas and can be used to assess the patient's psychology-mindedness. The therapist may also ask the patient how he or she understands some perplexing piece of behavior, give a trial interpretation, or begin an evaluation session by asking the patient whether he or she had any thoughts about the previous session. These techniques begin to establish a collaborative relationship with the patient and also provide information on the patient's wish to understand and his or her ability to use understanding as a modality to change behavior.

If the patient has had psychotherapy before, it is always important to understand the nature of the previous treatment. Earlier treatment experiences form the initial expectations the patient brings to any new treatment. Additionally, understanding the relationship with the former therapist clarifies how the patient expects the therapist to act and can be used to identify future transference paradigms.

Psychodynamic evaluation is a core skill. It is of importance to many psychiatric interventions other than the assessment for psychodynamic psychotherapy and is essential to the well-trained general psychiatrist. The psychodynamic doctor-patient conversation always has special characteristics, whether the goal is evaluation, long-term therapy, short-term therapy, pharmacotherapy, or any other form of intervention; and developing the skill to talk in this way is a complex part of the experience of becoming a psychiatrist. What follows are examples of psychodynamic evaluations for the student beginning to learn about this important technique. This process should also be integrated with both the overall evaluation and the process of psychodynamic listening.

Learning to do all this is a tall order, and in the pages that follow, examples of some of these tasks are provided. Yet this chapter is at best a brief summary of a process that can only be mastered by years of practice, many of which, optimally, should take place under the supervision of experienced psychodynamic clinicians.

■ THE CHIEF COMPLAINT

Unlike the case in many other medical situations, evaluating a new patient's chief complaint can involve probing for the unconscious meaning of what brings a person for help. This is certainly different, in a dramatic way, from what a person complains about when he has fallen and broken a bone and visits an orthopedic surgeon for treatment of a fracture. However, even in such a simple example there is an exception that needs to be stated clearly: a patient who returns repeatedly with fractures is communicating something about his state of mind, perhaps a recklessness or absence of judgment that keeps getting him into dangerous situations. But the surface message when a patient sees a psychiatrist is even more manifestly demanding of probing and interpretation, as the following example illustrates.

A 50-year-old woman sought consultation because she could not get along with her 22-year-old daughter and wanted advice from a mental health professional. The psychodynamic psychiatrist asked her new patient, in their very first session, to tell him all she could about her daughter and what she thought was going on at this time. The woman reported that her daughter had moved to a nearby city—about a hundred miles away—and had taken a job as a waitress to support her career as an aspiring actress. The woman went on to describe her daughter's outstanding dramatic education at a leading university. She knew that it was usual for young performers to support themselves by working at menial jobs, but she couldn't get it out of her head that her daughter shouldn't have to do that. She suddenly began to sob as she spoke, and the psychiatrist had the intuition that the suddenness and intensity of her tears suggested that they had appeared in response to something unspoken: her powerful emotion did not match her tone as she had been describing her daughter's situation.

The psychiatrist asked her patient whether something else on her mind made her feel so unhappy, and she burst out that with her daughter leaving, her nest was now empty. She said at once that this wasn't all bad, because in anticipation of it she had been speaking with the schools in her town about resuming her career as a librarian. She had even taken courses in the use of the computer in library work, so her own knowledge base was up to date. But, she added, despite all her past experience it seemed she would have to resume her career at the lowest level, as an assistant librarian in an elementary school. Twenty years before, she had retired as head of the local high school library, and she was disappointed that she could not just take up where she had left off, helping high school students learn to do library research.

The psychiatrist noted the parallel between her situation and the one she found so onerous in her daughter's life: underemployment at relatively menial tasks. The patient again began to sob, and during the next 15 minutes her chief complaint changed: she acknowledged a deep sadness and anger at her current job prospects. After she redefined her purpose in seeking consultation, it was decided to continue the psychodynamic evaluation with a new focus. Now the doctor and patient would recognize that this woman's own life situation was what was troubling her and that potential remedies for the sadness she experienced as she tried to reenter the workforce were her ultimate goal. They then settled on a plan to conduct four more evaluation interviews.

■ THE HISTORY OF THE PRESENT ILLNESS, THE PAST HISTORY, AND THE FAMILY HISTORY

Continuing the case study above, the psychiatrist noted at this point that this patient had employed a symbol in describing her own life situation, and she pointed this out to her patient: the patient had spoken of her daughter when she wanted to describe something about herself. The patient responded that she realized she had done this, and that she could imagine she expressed herself symbolically in many situations. She added that as an avid reader she was familiar with the use of symbols as a method of communicating. This was valuable information to the psychiatrist as she and her patient continued their exploration.

In subsequent sessions the psychiatrist asked the patient to describe the evolution of her present state of mind. The patient responded that she had been struggling to maintain her equilibrium for some time as her children grew up. The daughter about whom she had already spoken was her youngest, but over the past 5 years an older son and an older daughter had previously left home. All three children seemed well launched, but as each went out on his or her own, she was aware that she experienced a sense of loss and sadness that she couldn't fully understand. The psychiatrist wondered if she could describe her sadness, and the patient responded that throughout these years she had known that she was happy for her children, and she had felt proud of them and the job she had done raising them, yet she found herself missing them. The psychiatrist wondered to herself whether this patient was actually clinically depressed; but in the course of inquiring about various symptoms of depression, the psychiatrist determined that the patient was not depressed and was certainly not suicidal. In fact, the psychiatrist also determined that the patient could handle anger and other forms of aggression effectively: she had previously described anger over her job situation, and now she could even describe anger at her children for being less than sensitive about keeping in touch with her. Thus, she did not seem to be a person who for some psychodynamic reason was predisposed to turning anger against herself and becoming depressed or acting self-destructively in response to that dynamic.

Further exploration of the present illness reconfirmed that the patient's complaint about sadness and anger focusing on her employment situation was critical. Her relationship with her children did have a place in the picture: during the 20 years she had raised them and had not worked, she derived much pleasure from their accomplishments and felt consistently happy. Indeed, it was the happiest time of her life, for she enjoyed mothering, was blessed with talented children, and felt that the pressure to achieve on her own, always troubling to her in the past, had been lifted. Further, her husband of 30 years had been encouraging to her in her decision to be a full-time mother, and their relationship had grown in closeness and intimacy. So the psychiatrist began to develop a hypothesis: the patient's difficulties had to do with her own achievements, her own sense of self-esteem. When she was again forced to achieve on her own, her sensitivity to disappointment led to her unhappiness. The psychiatrist's inquiring about this led to a focus on the family history.

The patient described her high-achieving family of origin: two older sisters were outstanding in every way, and her parents, too, were both respected professionals, who showered praise on their three girls when they did well. Unfortunately, when they did not, criticism was severe, and the patient grew up in constant fear of disappointing her parents and feeling the withdrawal of their praise. She now related a repetitive dream to her psychiatrist, which she had had throughout her life since her teens. She was in school and was about to take an examination when she realized that she had not attended class all semester and would surely flunk. She felt deflated in the dream, angry at her teachers for not being more helpful to her during the school year, and very much disappointed in herself. The psychiatrist asked the patient what she thought about the dream. The patient responded that she thought it showed that she was not only fearful of failure, and ready to feel badly about herself when she was not successful, but angry at her parents for not being more encouraging to her as she grew up. From this discussion the psychiatrist learned that her patient could work with dreams, that she was aware of anger at her parents and able to deal with that state of mind, and that her problem with self-esteem had been an organizing aspect of her psyche since her childhood.

At this point much was known about this patient, and the psychiatrist was able to construct a psychodynamic formulation, using the four psychodynamic perspectives. In this formulation, the patient was seen as being guided by the wish for self-esteem, with defensive structures that allowed for a subjectively satisfactory adaptation, as long as she could look to others to achieve for her. She did not need to place herself on the competitive front line; she could let her children do that for her, and she could derive satisfaction and peace of mind through her identification with them. But their departure had brought to the fore her need to constantly shore up her sense of herself in the absence of memories of enduring and unconditional parental approval that could have helped her to feel good about herself most of the time.

This formulation, of course, created a picture of this patient's object relations, as well as the state of her self-esteem, wishes, and defenses. At that point, the psychiatrist believed that she had a good preliminary understanding of this patient and that the patient had the psychological needs (a problem of long-standing duration that reflected the patient's basic personality structure) and assets (the ability to engage in a self-explorative dialogue) consistent with embarking on a course of individual psychodynamic psychotherapy. But the psychiatrist wanted to assess in a tentative way how this patient's capacity for self-observation might hold up when a transference-countertransference situation evolved.

To do this, in the fifth and final evaluation session the psychiatrist asked how the patient felt about the four previous conversations they had had. Here the patient revealed that at times she had felt that she had displeased the psychiatrist by not being perceptive enough about herself. The psychiatrist suggested that this was an example of how the patient's characteristic way of experiencing herself in relation to others had found its way into the consulting room. The psychiatrist added that, from what she had heard of the patient's history, the psychiatrist believed that the patient usually had such feelings of low self-esteem in important relationships. The patient confirmed this, and the psychiatrist now explained to the patient that in psychodynamic psychotherapy what had just occurred was central to the work: when characteristic feelings were experienced in the relationship between patient and doctor, it was assumed they were a replaying of past feelings from important past relationships and that in a vivid way they could be explored and understood even as they were felt. That made sense to the patient, and the psychiatrist now felt that she could recommend a course of psychodynamic psychotherapy with the expectation that it would be very helpful to the patient. She did, the patient agreed to the recommendation, and they began what was to be a 3-year course of successful twice-weekly psychotherapy.

■ EARLY MEMORIES AND TRAUMA

In the previous example a woman sought help and was found to be a good candidate for psychodynamic therapy. In this example you will read about a man who had been in weekly psychotherapy for more than a year without relief of his symptoms.

> The patient was in his early thirties and had started therapy because of multiple fears: of crowds, going over bridges, air travel, driving in cars, using elevators. These symptoms had been there in a minor way since childhood, but in recent years they had worsened, and he had a general awareness of increasing anxiety all the time. There were no acute anxiety attacks, but there were obsessional rituals in which the patient felt forced to engage when he felt anxious. These included washing his hands, urinating before driving in his car (no matter how short the trip or the interval since he had previously urinated), and picking up stones from the dirt road in front of his house—in fear that if he did not, one would fly up as a car drove over it, enter the car through an open window, and injure someone.
>
> The patient had gone for a psychiatric evaluation and had been referred for cognitive-behavior therapy, which had not worked. When a benzodiazepine was added after a few months, there was likewise no relief. Finally, the patient sought help from a psychiatrist well trained in psychodynamic evaluation, who performed a reevaluation.
>
> This series of five sessions focused on the presenting complaint, the history of the present illness, the past history, and the family history. The patient said that when he was a child of about 7, he had first experienced obsessional symptoms and anxiety. He had been fearful of going to school and of stepping on cracks in the sidewalk. Those symptoms had lasted for a couple of years

and had abated on their own, although he had been left with the mild phobic symptoms already described. The present set of complaints had begun a couple of years ago, but the patient could not at first identify a precipitating event.

The psychiatrist asked the patient whether anything had occurred in his family at that time. The patient wondered aloud about the fact that around that time his father had become ill. His back had started to give him trouble, and he had required back surgery, which had been successful. Also at that time, his mother, always an anxious person, had become very frightened and had turned to the patient for help, which he had been able to provide in the form of reassurance. The clinician then inquired about the patient's family—its current configuration and past history—and about the patient's childhood and developmental history. The patient first commented that no one had asked him about this before and that perhaps it was of importance. What he next related took the psychiatrist by surprise, first because it had not been previously brought into focus, and then because of how the patient discussed it.

The patient said that he was an only child. He had recently moved out of his family home, because he was now doing well in his job with a large real estate development and management company. He was and had always been close to his parents and enjoyed Sunday dinner with them. He had a girlfriend and was planning to become engaged, and both his parents liked her very much. His parents and his maternal grandparents had migrated from Asia shortly before his birth and had lived together in the family home, prospering in a series of retail businesses. When he was born, everyone showered him with affection, he had been told, and he even remembered being the center of attention at his birthday party at the age of 5. The psychiatrist asked the patient to relate his earliest memory, and he reported that his earliest distinct memory was of his grandmother's taking ill shortly before that party and of an ambulance's coming for her and taking her to the hospital.

The patient then spontaneously reported that his grandmother had remained ill for the next couple of years, first with heart problems and then with some form of lymphatic cancer. During this time his mother had been very anxious, and the patient added without much feeling that perhaps it had not been such a happy time for him, as well, because his preoccupied mother had become progressively less available to him. The psychiatrist asked him to say what he meant by his mother's being preoccupied, and he explained that she had been very devoted to her mother and had worried about her all the time, devoting herself to her care at home.

Then the patient said that something did "sort of stand out in my mind" about that time in his life. He was reluctant to think much about it or believe that it could be very important, because "really" he had had such a wonderful childhood, with parents so hard-working and devoted to him. But he thought perhaps he should talk about it. One day when he was about 7, he returned home from school, and his parents and grandfather were at work. His grandmother, though ill, was in a stable state and was there to greet him when he got off the bus and to give him milk and cookies. She did so and then left the room. About half an hour later the patient called to her, and she did not answer. After calling several times, and getting no response, he got up from the table and went around looking for her. He found her collapsed in the living room, and he recalled that he had been unable to arouse her, had become very frightened, and had run out of the house looking for help. He found it at a neighbor's home: his parents were called, they rushed home, and again, an ambulance took his grandmother to the hospital. This time she never returned, dying a couple of weeks later. In retrospect, the patient said, his mother then had become very unhappy and had mourned for a long time, and he "guessed" that that was when he had developed his school phobia and his reluctance to step on cracks in the sidewalk.

He then had what he called a "curious" thought. There was a childhood rhyme that came into his head, "Step on a crack, break your mother's back." The psychiatrist asked what this meant to him, and he could not come up with anything. The clinician wondered if perhaps he was just now unconsciously fearful of learning something about himself: that he was so afraid of going to school and stepping on sidewalk cracks back then because underneath his conscious fears was the unconscious fear of wanting to hurt his mother. This was possible, the psychiatrist added, because, although he grew up in a devoted and loving family, at that time maybe he didn't feel so happy, and maybe he felt quite angry, too. The patient said that he had never thought of that, but that it made sense. In fact, he believed that possibly he had always felt some responsibility for his grandmother's collapse, maybe even for her death, as preposterous as he now knew this was. And, he added, if he felt responsible for that, he supposed he might have felt responsible for his mother's prolonged unhappiness after her mother had died. But "why angry?" he wondered.

To that question the psychiatrist responded with a question of his own: "Can you imagine why you might have been angry at your mother at that time?" The patient responded that he had been very close to his grandmother and that he had been very upset that he could not help her when she collapsed. He added that he had had no chance to speak of his upset to anyone and that he had carried it around with him for many years. The psychiatrist suggested that this might be reason enough to be angry with his mother: she had been unavailable to talk with him about his feelings. At this point the patient noted that perhaps that was why he had developed the symptom of a school phobia at the age of 7, along with the fear of stepping on cracks: it made sense to him that he hadn't wanted to leave his mother's side, as he had left his grandmother's side when she had collapsed. He had been so angry at his mother that he had felt he needed to be with her to protect her from some feared but wished-for punishment. He had also kept hoping she would start listening to him.

The patient then noted that he had always had a sense of responsibility to the members of his family and that his current symptoms might be related to the same sort of situation as his childhood symptoms. Now, as then, a family member had been ill, and his mother had been very upset. Perhaps he felt angry again, because when his father was ill he worried, too, and he could not get support from his mother but was expected only to be there to give her support. He noted that his symptoms might symbolically be ways of expressing his need to control his rage at his mother—to protect her from an unconscious wish he had to see her punished for not taking care of him—even though now, as an adult, those needs were in reality greatly diminished.

At this point the psychiatrist believed he knew an enormous amount about his patient. This young man could think psychologically and could step back from his emotional pain and examine the way his life history created the foundation for his psychiatric illness. He could appreciate the role of symbolism in the creation of his symptoms, as well as the role of a series of specific traumatic events involving his grandmother's illness and death and his mother's reactions to them, in shaping his personality and predisposing to his current reaction to an illness in his family. The clinician understood the role of aggressive wishes and impulses, largely unconscious, in his patient's current life and the need for this patient to employ defenses to prevent the conscious awareness of those wishes. That this patient had a solid sense of himself, and the capacity to regulate his self-esteem, was evident; the psychiatrist considered this an important factor in allowing this man to observe himself so well. Further, the psychiatrist believed that the patient had highly developed capacities to relate well to those around him and to develop intrapsychic structures reflecting those relationships. There were excellent adaptive capacities, despite the patient's difficulty in recognizing his own aggressive feelings. All this convinced the psychiatrist, too, that this man would be able to examine what might emerge in a transference relationship. He speculated to himself that the transference might take the form of the patient's feeling that the psychiatrist was not there to listen to him, as his mother had not been. This feeling, however, he did not share with the patient for fear of creating by suggestion a central transference configuration that might otherwise never emerge.

The clinician explained his findings to the patient and suggested that he was very capable of benefiting from psychodynamic therapy and that it could be conducted in various ways. The goal was up to the patient. If he felt that his difficulties handling his angry feelings were sufficiently pervasive, he might want more extensive therapy, with more sessions each week, in order to become less inhibited and more active in his life. If he felt that this difficulty was relatively untroubling, he might try briefer, less extensive therapy. The patient chose a trial of once-weekly psychodynamic psychotherapy, which after a year terminated successfully.

■ DEVELOPMENTAL DEFICIT

In the two cases so far described the patients were found during evaluation to be good candidates for psychodynamic psychotherapy, and in both cases that form of therapy proved beneficial. But that is not always the case, as this example illustrates.

A man in his forties came for evaluation. He lived alone, and he complained that he worked at a sales job that did not require nor reflect his educational accomplishments and that he felt sad and stuck in his life. The psychiatrist proposed that they meet several times to conduct an extensive evaluation. What emerged was that this man was the second of two children, his older sister having left for college when he was in high school. There she had met her husband. She had never returned home and now had a successful professional career and a family of her own. In contrast, the patient had lived at home all through college, continued a pattern of having no friends and no dating life, and spent most of his time alone.

The psychiatrist attempted to get a picture of what his patient's childhood had been like and learned that he had always felt socially awkward and had always spent a great deal of time with his mother. The psychiatrist wondered why that was the case, and the patient stated that he really didn't understand the reason, but that it seemed to him that both he and his mother preferred it that way. He added that in his early memories of being with his mother he didn't feel great, but it was at least better than feeling so shy around other children. He learned well in school but always preferred to go right home afterward.

He added that his parents had been close and that he had felt moderately close to them. After he finished school he got his own apartment, which his parents had encouraged him to do. A few years before, his parents had retired to another part of the country, and the patient had thought about moving there. But he had been unable to find a job and had decided to stay put. His life now consisted of working, watching television, and going to occasional movies.

The psychiatrist was struck with the emptiness of this patient's life, but he satisfied himself that this did not reflect an acute depression. He was also impressed with this patient's lack of imagination—his inability to think about his existence in terms of symbols in ways that might suggest that he saw his life as reflecting old patterns being replayed symbolically in the present. In fact, he was very concrete and very literal in the way he thought about everything. He saw his memories of the past as simply depicting his lifelong situation of an aloneness that he believed was his only option. Even dreams were taken literally: a dream in which he was alone was described as a reflection of his unhappy state, and there was no evidence of any idea that behind his aloneness there might be some wish to remain that way or some conflict over a wish to connect with others. He said he would probably be happy to live closer to his mother, but he couldn't see moving because there were few jobs where she now lived. He seemed to have no sense that perhaps he even harbored a secret preference to not connect with her.

The psychiatrist concluded that what he was seeing was rooted in this man's developmental experience, perhaps determined to a great extent by constitutional factors. There had been a profound failure to develop skills involving socialization, autonomy, the ability to define wishes and actualize them, the ability to relate to others, and the ability to define and sense one's own self. The patient, the psychiatrist concluded, had a serious developmental defect. But the psychiatrist wanted to give this man every chance he could; and the psychiatrist did recognize that there was some motivation for change, evidenced by the patient's decision to seek therapy. The patient had also gone through college and was certainly reasonably bright, although not gifted or insightful.

The psychiatrist believed that there was a good chance that insight-oriented, psychodynamic psychotherapy would founder on the rocks of this man's concreteness—his lack of imagination—and perhaps, too, on the likelihood that he, the psychiatrist, would be bored. As for the transference, to the extent that it would be seen by the patient concretely as a reflection of the barrenness of his life, it would probably be outside the realm of examination. To the extent that he might feel somewhat at ease in therapy, as he had with his mother, a relationship with a psychiatrist could be exploited therapeutically: the transference relationship could be a source of some solace in an otherwise profoundly empty life.

In consideration of all these factors, the psychiatrist recommended in a friendly fashion that he and the patient meet weekly and talk and see where their conversations led. Thus began a dialogue that lasted for 10 years. Surprisingly, as the years passed, the two of them grew closer than the psychiatrist had ever expected. The patient came to understand that he had received little understanding in childhood, and the willingness of the therapist to try to fathom his shyness helped him take a few steps toward connecting with others. He got in touch in a very tentative way with resentment toward his mother for not being better able to connect with him emotionally and with the idea that maybe he had really preferred to live far from her because of anger at her. He also learned how frightened he was in social situations of not knowing what to say, of being unsure of how to relate to others; and, using his conversations with his therapist as his model, he developed a small amount of confidence in his ability to be with others. The regularly scheduled therapy sessions ended when he had formed two friendships—one with a man, one with a woman with whom he went to the movies on Saturday nights. He actually imagined that someday he and his woman friend might have a sexual relationship, and to the extent that he wanted to, he discussed this before ending weekly therapy.

This largely supportive therapy had been informed by psychodynamic understanding of the powerful effects of developmental deficit, as well as by the potential for growth provided by a long-term new relationship with an understanding therapist. And although regular sessions were no longer held, a few times each year the patient and the therapist met in sessions to talk. They both knew that as long as both were alive, the meetings would continue.

■ CONCLUSION

In this chapter three examples of psychodynamic evaluation and history taking have been provided. Each is different; each had a different outcome. In these examples the elements of the psychodynamic evaluation have been touched upon, but at best this discussion is but an introduction to a process of great complexity. It is that which needs to be emphasized. The clinician able to perform a psychodynamic evaluation has mastered a complex skill, one that involves not only a knowledge of clinical syndromes, many psychological perspectives, and an understanding of human development but also the ability to relate empathically to another and use that relationship as a tool of assessment. To develop skill in this technique involves extensive training and experience under skilled supervision and the development of a deep understanding by the clinician of herself or himself.

An appreciation of one's own psychodynamics is of inestimable help as a model for understanding the psychodynamics of another human being, as a preventive for confusing what goes on in the mind of another with what goes on in the mind of the clinician, and as a tool for understanding the transference-countertransference situation. Help in understanding those personal dynamics can be obtained in a personal psychoanalysis or psychotherapy, in the practice of self-reflection, from the experience of supervision, and from the experience of intimate and regular consultation with experienced and trusted peers.

■ REFERENCES

1. Perry SW, Cooper AM, Michels R: The psychodynamic formulation: its purpose, structure and clinical application. Am J Psychiatry 144: 543–550, 1987
2. Horowitz MJ, Eells T, Singer J, et al: Role-relationship models for case formulation. Arch Gen Psychiatry 52:625–633, 1995
3. Malan DH: Toward the Validation of Dynamic Psychotherapy. New York, Plenum, 1980
4. Gabbard GO: Psychodynamic Psychiatry in Clinical Practice: the DSM IV Edition. Washington, DC, American Psychiatric Press, 1994
5. Gill MM, Newman R, Redlich FC: The Initial Interview in Psychiatric Practice. New York, International Universities Press, 1954
6. MacKinnon RA, Michels R: The Psychiatric Interview in Clinical Practice. Philadelphia, PA, WB Saunders, 1971

■ ADDITIONAL READINGS

McWilliams N: Psychoanalytic Diagnosis. New York, Guilford, 1994
Nemiah JC: Foundations of Psychopathology. New York: Jason Aronson, 1973
Tyson P, Tyson RL: Psychoanalytic Theories of Development: An Integration. New Haven: Yale University Press, 1990

6

BEGINNING TREATMENT

Psychodynamic psychotherapy is usually not a familiar form of medical treatment to the patient who is about to begin psychotherapy. At the end of the evaluation, the clinician discusses with the patient alternative forms of treatment that might in various ways be of benefit. In addition, the clinician must discuss with the patient how each of these treatments works. This approach is also true for psychodynamic psychotherapy. Psychodynamic psychotherapy can be explained to the patient as a process for learning a new method of problem solving, based on an understanding of the personal life history, the workings of the mind that are outside conscious awareness, and the personal view of the world—one's psychic reality. The individual's psychic reality hinges on the way in which past experience is used as an unconscious template for present behaviors— feelings, thoughts, fantasies, and actions.

Teaching the patient about the goals and process of psychodynamic psychotherapy is very important to the successful beginning of the psychotherapy. One way to conceptualize this phase of treatment is that an atmosphere of safety must be established (see Table 6–1). Although this may seem an imposing task, it is similar to the physician's task in many situations. For example, when the family practitioner finds that an otherwise healthy patient has a high cholesterol level, he or she must educate the patient and develop a cooperative working relationship so that together they can begin a treatment to counteract the potential ill effects of this silent condition.

In the opening phase of the treatment, the patient learns that

TABLE 6–1.	**Establishing the atmosphere of safety: the therapist's task**

Educate the patient about the past as a pattern for the present.

Educate the patient about the concepts of transference, defense, resistance.

Introduce and explain the abstinent role of the therapist.

Maintain the perspective of the concerned physician and forge the therapeutic alliance.

Deal with the patient's initial disappointment.

psychodynamic psychotherapy will work because in the relationship with the therapist, the patient will reexperience the past in the present through the transference relationship. By examining feelings in the therapy setting, the patient develops an understanding of how the personal past is continually reexperienced in life. The patient will then begin to understand that psychological pain can result from symbolically reliving the past in the here and now, causing the reawakening of the conflicted feelings and anxieties of childhood. The patient also learns by experience that through recognizing these unconscious processes, the painful feelings diminish and new behaviors are possible.

The patient is educated directly both through teaching and explaining and through example. At times, the clinician should explain very directly and supportively to the patient the process of the treatment. When this has been done, it is best not to continue to repeat the explanations but instead to change into a mode of understanding rather than teaching, listening to the patient's possible emotional blocks to understanding. The skilled clinician is always making decisions early in treatment about whether this is a time to educate or a time to listen to further material from the patient, delaying any further instructive comments. Generally the new therapist struggles with how much to educate and how much to listen in the opening sessions. Later in treatment, after explanations have been given clearly, the therapist can assume that cognitive education is not the difficulty the patient is having. But the therapist cannot assume this in the opening phase, particularly with the naive patient. Understanding the goals and processes of treatment is important to the patient's feeling safe and comfortable enough to explore and tolerate the anxiety that arises in the treatment setting (1–3).

■ ABSTINENCE AND FREE ASSOCIATION

After the patient has begun to understand the process of treatment, the therapist will, over time, become somewhat less verbally active in order to hear more about how the patient organizes her psychological world. Technically this is called being *abstinent*. Again the therapist may need to explain this to the patient if he or she asks about the therapist's silence. The therapist might say, "I am listening to you very closely. I want to be able to best understand how you see the world and not interfere with what you are telling me." The therapist also encourages the patient to speak as freely as possible and to suspend judgment about the accuracy or logic of what is said (see Table 6–2). This may be explained to the patient in the following manner: "You are free to say whatever you would like. In fact, it is most helpful if you say whatever comes to mind. I know that is difficult to do." The therapist assists the patient to say whatever comes to mind—to speak without editing thoughts—even though the patient may say things that she fears would be

---

TABLE 6–2. **Beginning treatment: the patient's task**

Develop a working alliance with the therapist.

Learn free association.

Appreciate the atmosphere of safety.

Recognize the disappointment of the opening phase.

Develop an understanding of transference, defense, and resistance.

Learn how to work with dreams, daydreams, and slips of the tongue.

---

untrue or hurtful to the therapist or to loved ones.

This method of communication is known as free association. It is characteristic of the mode of thinking and talking used by the patient in classical psychoanalysis. In psychodynamic psychotherapy the patient approaches this same state of mind. Although free association in classical psychoanalysis is much freer because of the other elements of the psychoanalytic treatment, the psychodynamic psychotherapy patient will come fairly close to that mode of expression (4).

Inevitably, free association is only relative, and the unconscious conflicts the patient experiences are the major forces that block the free expression of thoughts, feelings, and fantasies. The therapist in collaboration with the patient listens for clues to what may be outside the patient's awareness and may appear as a block to the free expression of thoughts. These ways of thinking that block uncomfortable feelings and conflicts from being experienced are called *defense mechanisms*. The therapist carefully observes, and at the right time shares with the patient, the patterns the patient shows in her thoughts and feelings and the blocks to these thoughts and feelings. The therapist observes the changes in the patient's thoughts and feelings and any movement away from the treatment. The therapist experiences the patient's defense mechanisms as a *resistance* to the work. Through the process of understanding how the resistances—the patient's defense mechanisms—operate, the transference emerges later in treatment.

The clinician and patient work together to recognize the patterns of the patient's thoughts and feelings. This collaborative work allows the patient to experience this task as one she can eventually assume, rather than as something magical. This task, the analysis of defenses, forms the basis on which the patient can eventually choose alternative behaviors. At times the enthusiasm of the new therapist can lead to wanting to tell the patient a pattern without working together with the patient to identify it. This can lead to the therapist's being seen as very powerful by the patient. Frequently this will create problems later in treatment.

The patient at times experiences feelings of frustration because of the clinician's relative silence. However, the patient should, overall, experience the therapist as standing with her, as an ally with whom he or she can master the forces that keep so much outside consciousness (5). Helping the patient understand this during the opening phase of treatment is essential. The patient who does not is much more likely to flee psychotherapy. Teaching all this quickly and understandably requires considerable skill, as illustrated in the following case study:

A married woman in her thirties came to a psychiatrist complaining of sadness since the death of her mother, 1 year before. She reported intermittent difficulty with sleeping and eating, although she had not lost weight. The woman asked for antidepressant medication, but the psychiatrist responded that there should be several meetings before a treatment approach was decided upon. The psychiatrist wanted to meet with his patient to observe how she related to him and to observe transference responses that might shed light on his patient's relationship with her deceased mother. He thought that possibly a psychodynamic explanation of her sadness might be identified and that subsequent psychotherapeutic efforts might work well for the patient.

He explained that he wanted to listen to how his patient's mind worked, that he would say little but listen attentively. The patient felt lost and bewildered and told this to the psychiatrist. He reassured her of his interest, but he otherwise remained silent. After the session the patient called her best friend who had herself worked with a psychotherapist a year before. The friend advised the patient to call the friend's former therapist, which the patient did.

A second consultation then took place with the

friend's psychiatrist. The second psychiatrist went about things differently. She explained in detail what she was looking for in the evaluation: a pattern of thought that would explain the patient's sadness, evidence of a psychobiological process of depression, or both. She explained the goals and process of psychodynamic psychotherapy, the nature of transference and how it could be studied, the nature of a safe therapy environment, and the usefulness of therapeutic abstinence and free association.

This time the patient decided to continue the evaluation, feeling comfortable and understood. After several sessions, during which the patient felt free to ask questions about the therapy and what they were doing together, and the psychiatrist felt free to answer them, the patient accepted a recommendation to embark on a course of twice-weekly psychodynamic psychotherapy. The patient had learned that her sadness about her mother's death was one of many feelings about her mother that she wanted to understand and that these feelings were often rooted in childhood. She felt confident in her therapist, felt safe with her, and could experience the therapist's abstinence as a useful therapeutic technique.

■ THE ATMOSPHERE OF SAFETY

Psychodynamic psychotherapy offers the patient a make-believe stage on which to play out the drama of his psychological life in an atmosphere of safety (5). In therapy, what the patient says is met with an effort to understand, not with judgment or criticism. The job of the psychodynamic psychotherapist does not involve managing the patient's life (one reason why patient selection is so important) nor judging its worth or the value of the way in which it is conducted (6).

The therapist's abstinent, neutral demeanor in the therapeutic setting is, in part, a contrivance, a technique, a special form of behavior designed to offer the patient the opportunity to "regress." Partly as a result of this unique aspect of the psychotherapeutic setting, and partly because of the normal course of life, the patient is able to think in a less well-organized, less structured fashion, giving access to more unconscious feelings and thoughts and thereby acting on the psychotherapeutic stage. Over time, the therapy becomes a laboratory in which the patient can examine in detail the feelings, thoughts, and fantasies he experiences toward another person (the therapist) in the safety of the therapeutic alliance.

Although this goal requires the therapist to be relatively passive and silent, this technical stance is not meant to be harsh or depriving. The collaboration develops in part through the clinician's appropriate concern and through explanations of the special kind of team effort and working together that are a part of the therapy. The therapist and the patient work together to understand the patient's experience, which in turn leads to the amelioration of his psychic pain. This common understanding developed between the patient and the therapist is sometimes referred to as a *contract*. However, this term tends to highlight the division of tasks and leaves out the most important part of the experience—the shared working together. The therapist and the patient are more accurately described as trying to develop a working (7), or therapeutic (8), alliance.

A medical student who was experiencing academic difficulty came for therapy. She immediately was tentative, wondering whether the psychiatrist could help her. The psychiatrist was naturally unsure and felt obliged to say this to the patient, but he did so in a way designed to create a safe atmosphere: "I don't know you well enough, yet, to even know what is wrong. Of course I can't reassure you, when I don't yet know you, that all will be well. I do know, however, that up to this point you have shown strengths, succeeding in college, getting into medical school. I can also imagine that now your world suddenly feels less safe, less predictable, since you are finding school very hard. I wonder, too, if right now you are feeling so vulnerable that you are afraid you won't have the right stuff to succeed as a patient, and that I'll be like a teacher and criticize you, kind of give you a low grade, rather than being your helper."

The patient began to sob and told the psychiatrist that his comments were very much what she was feeling. The psychiatrist responded that he was pleased and felt that he was now beginning to understand the patient and beginning to help her. The therapy was beginning in an atmosphere of safety and understanding, and the therapeutic alliance was forming.

■ THE ATTITUDE OF PHYSICIANLY CONCERN

A source of misunderstanding in the minds of many beginning psychodynamic psychotherapists is the degree to which the therapist should hide her own personality or humanity. A caricature that many beginning therapists possess as a model is of a blank-faced, unsmiling, unresponsive therapist, who remains silent for many minutes, or even many sessions. Once in a while this therapist offers a perfunctory pronouncement or an interpretation that cuts to the core of the patient's psyche.

In fact, this is not at all what the psychodynamic psychotherapist is like. She is not cold, aloof, or arbitrary. Nor is she withholding for the sake of being withholding, callous, or detached (9). Rather, the psychodynamic psychotherapist is relatively passive (or abstinent) in order to create a therapeutic environment that permits the patient to become aware of hidden wishes and conflicts.

The psychiatrist doing this form of therapy works from the

perspective of the concerned physician, with gentleness and an awareness of the patient's pain (5, 9). Over and over again, through working together, the physician conveys the awareness that the patient is experiencing psychological pain not only in life outside the therapy but, because of reexperiencing the past, in life inside the therapy as well. The psychiatrist conveys respect for the patient's efforts to understand himself and to keep going in therapy in spite of the pain.

The following example illustrates the patient's awareness of this atmosphere of physicianly concern:

> A single man in his late thirties came for psychiatric evaluation because of frequent attacks of anxiety about his performance at work. Although he was a highly educated professional, he had had no previous contact with a psychiatrist and had no understanding of how psychodynamic psychotherapy worked. After a thorough evaluation, he started treatment, and several months later made the following observation to his psychiatrist: "I now know why you don't speak to me more freely, the way you did during the evaluation. You want me to come in here and speak freely, to say what's on my mind. When I do that I always seem to get in touch with feelings that feel like they belong to the past, feelings I had toward friends and adults when I was growing up. I think if you answered all my questions, or responded to me immediately, we wouldn't know what was on my mind, and we wouldn't get at those feelings. Because we do, I am getting to know myself better, to understand how I became who I am."

■ DISAPPOINTMENT IN THE OPENING PHASE

During the opening phase the patient first encounters various aspects of the psychotherapeutic situation. The therapist orients the patient to these events and to how they can be used to advantage. Often, the first specific reaction encountered by the patient is a sense of disappointment when the therapist becomes more abstinent. In part this reaction occurs because, no matter how carefully the therapist attempts to prepare the patient, the patient experiences a loss of the emotional support that characterized the evaluation. In addition, the first flush of magical hope that so often surrounds beginning treatment soon fades, leaving most patients with a sense of confusion, frustration, and helplessness. "How will this psychiatric treatment help?" they wonder, sometimes aloud, but more often just on the edge of their awareness. Because the psychiatrist has been invested with authority and expertise by the patient, when the therapist becomes quieter and the patient is thus asked to work more independently, feelings are usually reawakened from past situations in which the individual was asked to take steps toward psychological maturity.

Thus, for example, it is as if the patient were again progressing in school or as if he were being asked to assume more responsibility despite his fears of injury or failure. Some variation on this theme is almost inevitable. The therapist uses this occurrence to enhance the patient's understanding of how therapy brings to consciousness feelings from the past. This is often the patient's first opportunity to see the therapy in action and learn from doing. This initial disappointment is illustrated in the following case:

> A patient in her late twenties took a job in a distant city after debating the move for a year. She left behind her family of origin and her friends, and she found herself depressed and anxious in her new home and her new work. She sought psychiatric assistance, and after a period of evaluation she began psychodynamic psychotherapy. During the second month of twice-a-week therapy she began to feel more depressed and was concerned that her psychiatrist was not being helpful to her.

The therapist responded to this feeling with concerned inquiry. The patient revealed that during the months before leaving home she had sought advice from her parents about what to do. But no matter what they said, she felt dissatisfied. The psychiatrist wondered whether her leaving home represented an effort to become more independent and to grow psychologically, adding that this effort might also have caused the patient to worry about being on her own and about her own well-being. The patient agreed. This exchange was a good start for the therapy, for thereafter, when the patient became worried that her psychiatrist was not involved enough or not giving her enough advice, the therapist and patient together were able to refer to this initial episode and explore the patient's current desires for growth and her fears of the challenges and consequences of this growth.

■ THE EARLY EXPERIENCE OF TRANSFERENCE, DEFENSE, AND RESISTANCE

The preceding example, which involves the development of the working relationship, or *alliance* (7, 8), also brings up the issue of transference. Transference is at the core of how psychotherapy works, but it is never easily understood by the patient. Freud developed the idea that all human relationships are transference relationships. By this he meant that all human beings experience others by superimposing their perceptions of figures from the past on new individuals. Today, although within psychoanalysis there exists a range of views on the nature of transference, it is generally felt that memories of the past are activated in all relationships. To some extent, each individual unconsciously plays out in current relationships certain aspects of important past relationships.

Because the psychodynamic psychotherapist is abstinent and

does not share details of her personal life with the patient, the therapist creates a kind of blank screen on which the patient may paint a transference picture of his or her own design. Early in the therapy this becomes apparent. By pointing it out, the therapist and the patient create a common focus of attention. In this way the patient's understanding of how therapy works is also deepened. The transference, which is related to the reaction of disappointment the patient experiences to the therapist's abstinence, is often very specific:

Early in treatment a patient noted that the therapist had on her wall a United Nations human rights poster. The patient expressed concern that this indicated that the psychiatrist was politically liberal, whereas he, the patient, was politically conservative. Inquiry by the therapist revealed that the patient was afraid that his aggressive view of American foreign policy would earn the disapproval of the psychiatrist, who would consider the patient insensitive and even bloodthirsty. The therapist listened, not to the concrete issue raised by the patient, but to the category of the patient's concern: the fear of disapprobation because of aggressive impulses.

The therapist commented to the patient that perhaps he was concerned that the therapist would disapprove of his being so aggressive. The patient responded that his mother had disapproved of his aggressiveness and he worried a good deal about the psychiatrist's attitude toward him. The therapist noted to herself that such reactions might again be played out in the patient's responses to her, and as the therapy progressed, transference feelings along these lines became prominent. This interaction in the beginning of treatment served as a foundation that allowed the patient and the psychiatrist to work together to explore these feelings more deeply as

the treatment progressed, with the patient's understanding of the process that was occurring.

The psychotherapist attempts to clarify the patient's feelings
and the meaning of what the patient is trying to say. At other times,
the therapist may supportively confront the patient with attitudes
the patient has disavowed but clearly demonstrates. In both cases
the therapist is hoping to point out the kinds of thoughts and
feelings that the patient obscures and the ways they are obscured,
defended against, and kept unconscious. Throughout this process
the patient's defensive ways of thinking are elucidated. The ex-
treme of the patient's defenses is evident when the patient wants to
quit the treatment prematurely. This event may be disturbing to the
beginning therapist, who may have invested a great deal in a first
long-term case. The therapist's attitude of treating the wish to stop
treatment as another defense to be understood compassionately and
to be explored for its developmental roots may often allow this
defense to be understood and may allow the patient to feel relief
and continue treatment.

In the opening phase the therapist will have the opportunity to
identify patterns of defense and resistance and must orient the
patient to how awareness of these patterns can be used to advance
the patient's knowledge of herself. In particular, there are certain
categories of thoughts and feelings that are difficult for most
patients to recognize in themselves and to share with others. Often
kept unconscious by defensive thinking, these feelings include
self-doubt, self-hatred, helplessness, rage at others, and affection
for others.

A middle-aged man completed an evaluation and began
psychotherapy with a female psychiatrist. From the start
this man had a difficult time talking in his therapy. His
50-minute sessions were often characterized by substantial periods of silence, lasting up to 10 minutes. After

drawing the patient's attention to his silences, the therapist, recognizing the silence as a resistance, inquired
whether during these silences he was experiencing
thoughts about her. The patient was at first embarrassed
by this question. The therapist responded with an understanding comment and the reassuring assertion that
whatever he was thinking was important in advancing
their collaborative efforts. He then noted that he found
her very attractive. He went on to say that because she
had brought up the possibility of his having thoughts
about her, he was able to bring them into the open.

In this example the patient's thoughts were about the psychiatrist; but of course this is not always the case. They may be about
anyone or any subject. Nevertheless, often the patient's thoughts
will be about the therapist, no matter what troubles the patient
brings to the therapy. This is true because the patient wants very
much to forge a relationship with the therapist to be relieved of his
suffering and also because of the phenomenon of transference. It is
essential for the therapist to listen empathically to whatever transference thoughts and feelings the patient might express and to work
with the patient to understand them in depth (10).

■ INITIAL USE OF DREAMS IN THERAPY

The therapist also attends to the dream life of the patient. Not all
patients in psychotherapy work extensively with dreams, but many
do, and for those who can, the work is an important tool. Every
patient should be given the opportunity to work with dreams. It is
in the opening phase that this road to understanding is introduced
and learned. Frequently, dreams reported early in treatment are
particularly revealing of the core conflicts of the patient. They can
also serve to educate the patient about unconscious processes.
Later in treatment, the mechanisms of defense often make dreams
more difficult to understand.

The following case illustrates a dream occurring early in treatment:

The patient was a young woman, recently divorced, who was depressed and anxious. In the third week of twice-weekly psychodynamic psychotherapy she reported that the previous night she had gone to bed thinking about her session the next day. She had had affectionate thoughts about her female therapist as she fell asleep. In her dream she saw two airplanes flying high in the sky. The smaller one was running out of fuel, and the second one, much larger, sent forth a fuel line, which entered the smaller plane, replenishing its fuel supply. But then something went wrong; the refueling apparatus did not work. The patient awoke, fearful that the smaller plane would crash.

At this early phase of the patient's therapy, this dream, so ripe with symbolism, could not be understood in depth. The psychiatrist had many hypotheses: that the dream symbols represented the patient's view that her therapy might become a situation of nurturance gone awry—a disappointment; that the dream symbols represented the patient's view of her marriage gone awry—her failed heterosexual life; that the dream reflected masochistic wishes, born out of guilt-provoking wishes regarding needs for gratification. But the therapist recognized that most of these ideas were merely hypotheses and could be neither supported nor rejected with the available data. She chose to use this as a time to explain to the patient that dreams were a way of thinking while asleep and could indicate concerns one had—present and past. Rather than introduce the patient to dream work per se, the therapist chose to interest the patient in her unconscious processes. She commented to the patient that perhaps the dream was related to an unspoken fear the patient had, since she fell asleep while thinking about her therapist: that this helpful woman would fail her or disappoint her, and that as a result she would feel her life was in danger. To this the patient agreed and went on to say that she felt that her husband had abandoned her and disappointed her terribly and that her divorce had left her feeling very vulnerable.

In the course of her therapy, which lasted several years, this patient used her dreams effectively as a source of knowledge. She developed a transference in which she demonstrated that she felt close to women she perceived as nurturant and close to men she perceived as both kind and passionate. It became clear that these transference feelings were based on early life experiences and that in all such present-day relationships she felt guilty because she believed her demands were too great. It also became clear that she always felt vulnerable to disappointment in these relationships. She was eventually able to trace her tendency to expect disappointment back not only to her divorce but to her early life experiences. Certainly all this was, in retrospect, played out in the dream she had had at the start of her treatment.

■ REFERENCES

1. Jacobs T, Rothstein A (eds): On Beginning an Analysis. Madison, CT, International Universities Press, 1990
2. Abend S: The influence of the patient's previous knowledge on the opening phase, in On Beginning an Analysis. Madison, CT, International Universities Press, 1990, pp 57–66
3. Busch F: Beginning a psychoanalytic treatment: establishing an analytic frame. J Am Psychoanal Assoc 43:449–468, 1995
4. Freud S: Resistance and repression (1917), in The Standard Edition of the Complete Psychological Works of Sigmund Freud, Vol 16. Translated and edited by Strachey J. London, Hogarth Press, 1963, pp 286–302

5. Schafer R: The atmosphere of safety: Freud's "Papers on Technique" (1911–1915), in The Analytic Attitude. New York, Basic Books, 1983, pp 14–33

6. Poland WS: On the analyst's neutrality. J Am Psychoanal Assoc 32:283–299, 1984

7. Greenson RR: The working alliance and the transference neurosis. Psychoanal Q 34:155–181, 1965

8. Zetzel ER: Current concepts of transference. Int J Psychoanal 37:369–376, 1956

9. Stone L: Notes on the noninterpretive elements in the psychoanalytic situation and process. J Am Psychoanal Assoc 29:89–118, 1981

10. Gill MM: The analysis of the transference. J Am Psychoanal Assoc 27:263–288, 1979

■ ADDITIONAL READINGS

Blum HP: The curative and creative aspects of insight. J Am Psychoanal Assoc 27 (suppl):41–69, 1979

Curtis HC: The concept of therapeutic alliance: implications for the "widening scope." J Am Psychoanal Assoc 27 (suppl):159–192, 1979

Schwaber E: Psychoanalytic listening and psychic reality. International Review of Psycho-analysis 10:379–392, 1983

7

RESISTANCE AND DEFENSE

The terms *resistance* and *defense* refer to the forces within the patient that oppose the aims of treatment. When patients come for and work in dynamic psychotherapy, it is because they want relief from neurotic symptoms and because, rationally, they want to cooperate with a therapist whom they trust and respect. However, every patient, no matter how reasonable and how strongly motivated, is ambivalent about getting well. Emotional symptoms are associated with unconscious conflicts composed of traumatic memories, conflicted impulses, and painful affects. Some of the very forces that cause the patient's symptoms also work to prevent the conscious recovery of these memories, feelings, and impulses. These forces also work against the intentions of the therapy to bring the painful emotional contents into the patient's consciousness. Therapy always requires courage to face the emotional distress of reliving painful memories and feelings. So it is understandable that patients may be reluctant to undergo treatment.

■ RESISTANCE

Resistance is a general term referring to all the forces in the patient that oppose the painful work of therapy. There are many different categories of resistance, including general fear of any change, an overly harsh conscience that punishes a patient with the continuation of neurotic suffering, and the insistence on the gratification of childish impulses that forms part of an emotional illness. This last resistance is often seen in an erotic or a hate-filled transference.

The patient may have an erotic transference toward the therapist that he or she wishes to gratify rather than understand. The patient may have a hateful transference and wish to thwart the therapist instead of interpreting the sources of his or her own aggression. These last two examples are special forms of resistance, called "transference resistance," which are discussed later in this chapter. Another kind of resistance is a result of the dread of the experience and expression of powerful childish impulses that therapy might uncover.

The pleasures of acting out can also lead to resistance to treatment. Acting out is seen in the addictions and the perversions through which the patient gratifies the conflicted impulses. The patient is loath to contain and interpret these conflicted impulses. Acting out is also seen in more disturbed patients who may be impulsive. In the sway, for example, of a hostile or erotic transference to the therapist, such patients may find partners outside treatment with whom to enact their feelings instead of discussing, interpreting, and mastering these feelings in the therapy sessions. Acting out can also take place within the therapeutic relationship and during periods of intense emotions about the therapist. A patient may drive past the therapist's home or gather personal information about the therapist. This particular kind of acting out is another form of transference resistance.

The secondary gain from illness also leads to resistance to recovery. Some patients are so accustomed to the accommodations others have made and the special favors they receive by virtue of their being ill that they are unwilling to give up the "perks" of illness that recovery would entail. Further, the financial and emotional dependence that results from receiving psychiatric disability payments can be a formidable obstacle to recovery.

■ DEFENSE

All people, including patients in therapy, employ *mechanisms of defense* to keep painful feelings and memories outside conscious awareness. These defense mechanisms are specific, discrete maneuvers or ways of thinking that the mind employs to avoid painful emotional material. The patient's defense mechanisms are an important source of resistance in psychotherapy. In 1936, Anna Freud, in *The Ego and the Mechanisms of Defense* (1), outlined the functioning of many of these defense maneuvers. Since that time the list has grown and been elaborated on (see Table 7–1). The most common and important mechanisms of defense are given below.

Repression

Repression, among the first mechanisms of defense described by Sigmund Freud, refers to the active pushing out of awareness of painful memories, feelings, and impulses. For example, a hysterical patient suffering from sexual arousal disorder represses all feelings of sexual arousal and may also repress the memories of sexual feelings that led to conflicts in early childhood.

TABLE 7–1.   **Mechanisms of defense**

Common defense mechanisms	**Primitive defense mechanisms**
Repression	Splitting
Denial	Projection
Reaction formation	Projective identification
Displacement	Omnipotence
Reversal	Devaluing
Inhibition	Primitive idealization
Identification with the aggressor	
Asceticism	
Intellectualization	
Isolation of affect	
Regression	
Sublimation	

Denial

Denial, similar to repression, averts a patient's attention from painful ideas or feelings without making them completely unavailable to consciousness. A patient using denial simply ignores painful realities and acts as if they do not exist. Examples include the case of a deposed and disgraced leader who insists on continuing to pose as a respected statesman and the case of a family's avoidance of discussing an ill, dying relative to avoid the painful feelings evoked.

Reaction Formation

Reaction formation is seen to some degree in all patients and to a marked degree in patients with obsessive-compulsive disorder. It consists of exaggerating an emotional trend to help repress the opposite emotion. The obsessional patient may manifest punctuality, parsimony, and cleanliness to defend against wishes to be tardy, extravagant, and messy.

Displacement

Displacement is, simply, changing the object of one's feelings from the real object to a safer one. The worker who is enraged by his boss and comes home, abuses his dog, and shouts at his family is a familiar example. In the treatment situation, patients frequently displace the transference feelings they experience toward the therapist and express them toward other people in their lives. In their associations, when patients report their love, hate, anger, rivalry, etc., toward others, it is often the feelings toward the therapist that are being expressed.

Reversal

Reversal is changing an impulse from active to passive (and vice versa) or directing an impulse toward the self instead of toward another (or vice versa). Using active sadistic feelings to conceal less conscious masochistic wishes is a common example. Another is reproaching the self instead of expressing disappointment in someone else.

Inhibition

Inhibition is the constriction of thought or activity to avoid thoughts or activities that stir anxiety. Inhibition is frequently seen in phobic patients who avoid exposures such as heights, plane trips, or certain animals that comprise the phobic situation. It is also seen in patients who may, for example, inhibit assertiveness or sexual expression in order to avoid anxiety.

Identification With the Aggressor

This defense mechanism is the tendency to imitate what the patient perceives as the aggressive and intimidating manner of an external authority. Little children who are just learning to control their own impulses are severe critics of their peers in imitation and even caricature of the controlling parent. Patients may similarly mask their fear of a critical authority by adopting a hypercritical attitude.

Asceticism

Anna Freud identified asceticism as a mechanism of defense used especially by adolescents to control the pressure of the intense sexual feelings present after puberty. Asceticism is the denial of pleasures to oneself. This denial may involve food, sleep, exercise, or sexual gratification, all usually denied with an air of superiority and of doing something good for oneself.

Intellectualization

Intellectualization is a factual and excessively cognitive way of experiencing and talking about conflicted topics without feeling the associated affects.

Isolation of Affect

Isolation of affect, a defense related to intellectualization, is the repression of the feelings connected with a particular thought. Both intellectualization and isolation of affect are typical of obsessional patients in particular.

Regression

Regression is the return to earlier modes of psychosexual functioning to avoid the conflicts experienced at a later developmental stage. Regression to oral and anal concerns to avoid oedipal conflicts is a common clinical occurrence.

Sublimation

Sublimation is a mature mechanism of defense. It is the hoped-for, healthy, nonconflicted evolution of a primitive childhood impulse into a mature level of expression. For example, a painter or ceramist may use a sublimated wish to smear feces, a photographer may use sublimated voyeurism, and dancers and actors may use a sublimated form of exhibitionism. Political activism channels sublimated aggression. Healthy adult friendships are partly fueled by sublimated homosexual and incestuous impulses.

The more primitive mechanisms of defense—splitting, projection, projective identification, omnipotence, devaluing, and primitive idealization—are discussed in Chapter 14 and listed in Table 14–1.

■ INTERPRETING RESISTANCES AND DEFENSE MECHANISMS

In psychodynamic psychotherapy the therapist hopes to understand the unconscious conflicts that led to the patient's emotional symptoms. Conflict arises in the child when normal impulses are associated with unpleasant feelings, such as fear of punishment, disapproval, and disappointment. Each individual is born with her own constitutional givens—for example, the strength of drives and wishes and the capacity to tolerate frustration. Each individual also has a unique personal history rooted in interactions with parents, family, and other caregivers within her social structure and greater community. No one grows up without some conflicts—clashes between impulses and prohibitions—that are rendered unconscious by various defense mechanisms and can possibly give rise to neurotic symptoms.

In psychotherapy the therapist strives to interpret the defenses that obscure the old conflicts so that the patient can reexperience consciously the old forbidden impulses and memories and the fears, disappointments, and painful affects associated with them (see Table 7–2). The therapist detects the presence of resistance in the patient by a block in the patient's free association. This difficulty may be evidenced in a flow of trivial-sounding associations that seems a mere reporting of daily events and that does not seem to deepen in personal and emotional intensity and relevance. Resistance is also evidenced by a dampening or absence of affect, an atmosphere of boredom, an avoidance of emotionally charged details, or a patient's blocking and silence. Whenever a patient is manifesting resistance, in whatever form, it is because the patient is protecting himself or herself from remembering and reliving the old dangers and fears associated with forbidden impulses.

TABLE 7–2.   **Principles of interpreting resistance**

Acknowledge the contribution of reality to the resistance.

Respect resistances and defenses as evidence of a patient's character strengths.

Remember that the patient must recognize and experience the resistance before it can be interpreted.

Interpret the resistance before the content (the what or why of the patient's resistance).

Many resistances derive from the character structure of the patient. For example, an inhibited obsessional patient may veer away from painful material into a labored rendition of minute and trivial details while also isolating his affect. The patient is resisting the work of therapy by using his characteristic personality style with which he defends himself everywhere against anxiety. On the other hand, a patient with a histrionic personality style may be unable to give any precise details of emotionally significant events both because of the histrionic individual's typical use of repression and because of his impressionistic, vague way of experiencing events and processing information, typical of the histrionic patient.

A person's defenses, which lead to resistance in therapy, derive from the wish to avoid psychic pain and also from the adaptive strengths of a given character structure. The same hypothetical obsessional patient who isolates affect and who has available a flow of minutely detailed facts may be, for example, a neurosurgeon, an air traffic controller, or a pilot, capable of describing accurately and dealing unemotionally with situations of great tension while remaining clear about a myriad of important details. The hysterical patient with a vague or impressionistic way of relating events may also have a flair for acting, the arts, or other fields requiring emotionally intense functioning.

Character and defenses represent ways of structuring mental and emotional experience to keep psychic pain at a minimum and bring one's interpersonal and intrapsychic functioning and relationships into some congruence with external reality. The defenses of a particular character structure should be viewed by the clinician as a manifestation of the strength of the personality, central to adaptation and functioning. Although defenses seem to work against the uncovering work of dynamic psychotherapy by fueling resistance, they should be respected as important sources of information about a patient and slowly interpreted, not abruptly confronted. In the earliest days of psychoanalysis, Freud interpreted unconscious themes without regard for the patient's opposing defenses. He soon realized, however, that interpreting the unconscious material that the patient's defenses continue to reject does not lead to integration of the warded-off mental conflicts. Instead, the mental conflicts are immediately resubjected to the same defenses and again rendered unconscious.

For this reason, Freud formulated the rules still important in dynamic psychotherapy known as "interpreting resistance before content" or "interpreting from the surface down." What this means is that the therapist first points out a patient's resistances, drawing the patient's attention to them. Then the therapist inquires about the patient's need to be resistant at a particular moment. The therapist then can move on to determine what, specifically, the patient is defending against.

Recently, more modern theorists from several different psychodynamic schools have stressed anew the need for careful and consistent interpretation of resistances (2). A methodical approach to resistance has been emphasized, always interpreting the need for a resistance and the psychological dangers a patient needs to avoid. In this way, one helps the patient enlarge her capacity for viewing intrapsychic activity.

Self psychology, a modern viewpoint in psychodynamic thinking, departs from the traditional Freudian ideas of instinctual drives that become conflicted, repressed, and kept unconscious by defenses. For a self psychologist, the most important variable is a patient's sense of self and the degree to which the self feels cohesive or vulnerable to instability and fragmentation. From this perspective, defenses are not seen as barriers to discovering hidden conflicts. Rather, defenses are seen as crucial protections of a fragile self from weakening or further depletion (3). Therefore, defense interpretation is guided by the need to be vigilant about the patient's sense of safety and cohesiveness as defended feelings are interpreted. Similarly, the importance of empathy, or interpreting from the perspective of the patient's experience, as the necessary mode for analytic intervention has been emphasized in self psychology (4).

■ TRANSFERENCE RESISTANCE

In addition to resistance stemming from the typical defenses of a given patient's character style, there are several *transference resistances*. These resistances arise when a patient experiences powerful feelings toward the therapist. The feelings tend to take over the direction of the treatment, moving the patient away from the rational goal of uncovering and resolving the conflicts that led to his symptoms. Transference resistances originate from strong positive or negative transference attitudes. Patients with an erotic transference may wish to have a sexual relationship with the therapist or may become resistant in order to avoid the awareness of strong sexual feelings in the transference. More narcissistic and dependent patients may hunger for admiration, recognition, and support instead of insight. Feeling frustrated in his transference longings, the patient may become furious and retaliatory and refuse to cooperate for a time in order to thwart the therapist. Transference resistance is illustrated by the following case:

> A schoolteacher in psychodynamic psychotherapy had avoided, for a number of years, feeling any closeness to her therapist. After several weeks of unusual warmth toward the therapist, she came to her session in a mellow mood and spoke with pleasure about the antics of her new puppy. Suddenly she drew back and said, "Now I feel you're cut off from me. That's how I used to feel with my boyfriend, and it's also the distance I used to feel from my mother." In the initial months of treatment such an interruption in the feeling tone in the hour would have led to an emotional distancing that might have lasted for weeks. Now, after working for several years in treatment, the patient had considerable ability to work with her own resistances. She said, "I think I pulled back because you didn't laugh and share my pleasure about the puppy. My mother never empathized with my pleasures either, only

with the tragedies. She did laugh, sometimes, but it was more at me than with me. Mother would say that for a bright girl I could act pretty dumb."

Despite these important connections, the patient continued to be hostile and withdrawn because the therapist did not laugh about the puppy. She was in a state of transference resistance reflecting both the frustration of her loving impulses that she had felt and, more deeply, her fear of expanding her loving feelings. The therapist asked, "How did you feel here yesterday?" The patient responded, "Good. Oh, I see. Yes, I felt calm and warm toward you and that always makes me anxious. I swing back and forth between feeling close and having surges of anger with you. I feel I have to work so hard to pull you in and keep you engaged." The therapist asked, "Did you work hard like that to keep your mother's attention?" and the patient responded, "Yes, but I could never trust her attention and I could never keep it."

This brief episode of successfully interpreted transference resistance led to an important clarification of the patient's lifelong pattern of pursuing ambivalent and emotionally unavailable men. As in this example, transference resistance—and resistance in general—can both cause a crisis in therapy and, if successfully interpreted, be an opportunity leading to an understanding and reworking of conflicted and restricting patterns from the past.

This example also illustrates the very important topic of how to work with a patient's resistances. The therapist must first make a patient aware that he or she is resisting (5). It is impossible to work with a patient to interpret resistances if the patient feels the reactions are reasonable. Sometimes one must wait until a resistance becomes intense and obvious enough for the patient to acknowledge. The importance of the therapist's sense of timing is illustrated in the following two cases:

> A patient was consistently seven or eight minutes late for every appointment. He always had reasonable-sounding explanations for his tardiness, which the therapist understood as a resistance to the treatment. Only after several months of consistent and increasing lateness did the patient accept that his pattern was more than a choice. Only then could he consciously experience and acknowledge his anxiety and his wish to avoid his deepening feelings in the transference.

The first step of working with any resistance is to demonstrate to the patient that she is resisting. This must be done before any attempts are made to interpret what is being resisted and why.

> A patient with paranoid and schizoid features experienced an intensely hostile transference resistance and considered cutting back or interrupting her twice-weekly therapy sessions. She rationalized that the therapist was untrustworthy, was exploitative, and only wanted the patient's money. The therapist noted with the patient the appearance of the hostile mood. Later, the therapist noted to the patient that the appearance of the hostile mood had begun at the same time the patient had made gains that included a new job with increased pay and that culminated in her finally buying herself a home, all of which made the patient very anxious.
>
> The patient acknowledged that she was very nervous about buying a home. She was especially mistrustful that the people from whom she was purchasing the house would cheat her. In fact, she was very afraid, in general, of being cheated or harmed. She felt especially afraid that

an intruder would break in through a first-floor window as soon as she moved into her new home. The reasons for her anxiety became evident in a series of dreams that depicted the patient's life-and-death competitive struggle with her mother. Through the dreams the patient was able to reexperience her mother as simultaneously envious, devaluing, and possessive of her, like her experience with the therapist and her fears in buying the house. The patient feared her mother would both resent the patient's accomplishments and resist her increasing separateness and autonomy. The therapist had successfully drawn the patient's attention to the fact that she was resisting. Then, through the work with the dreams, the transference resistance was connected to this heightened anxiety.

In working with resistances, it is always important to respect defenses, to avoid arguing with patients, and to recognize the reality components of resistances before interpreting their unconscious motives (Table 7–2). For example, patients often plead limitations of time and money as difficulties in the way of treatment. These issues are real and often do represent obstacles to therapy. It is helpful to acknowledge the realities first before beginning an inquiry into the details and extent of such an impediment. With the obsessional patient it can be helpful to agree with the patient that the ability to think about details has been a great strength of the patient's. The therapist may then point out: "At times a very strong, hypertrophied muscle can also, however, interfere with other movements." Tact, respect, and maintaining an alliance with the reasonable part of the patient are key to working with resistances.

■ REFERENCES

1. Freud A: The Ego and the Mechanisms of Defense, Revised Edition. New York, International Universities Press, 1966

2. Gray P: The Ego and Analysis of Defense. Northvale, NJ, Jason Aronson, 1994
3. Ornstein A: Self-object transferences and the process of working through, in The Realities of Transference: Progress in Self Psychology, Vol 6. Edited by Goldberg A. Hillsdale, NJ, Analytic Press, 1988, pp 116–134
4. Schwaber E: Empathy: a mode of analytic listening, in Empathy II. Edited by Lichtenberg J, Bornstein M, Silver D. Hillsdale, NJ, Analytic Press, 1984
5. Greenson R: The Technique and Practice of Psychoanalysis, Vol 1. New York, International Universities Press, 1967

■ ADDITIONAL READINGS

Nemiah JC: Foundations of Psychopathology. New York, Oxford University Press, 1961
Sandler J, Dare C, Holder A: The Patient and the Analyst: The Basis of the Psychoanalytic Process. New York, International Universities Press, 1973
Shapiro D: Neurotic Styles. New York, Basic Books, 1965

8

TRANSFERENCE

Freud struggled to understand the concept of transference. Currently psychoanalysts believe that the founder of psychoanalysis saw transference as part of all human relationships. From this vantage point, transference is a concept of staggering importance. It postulates that not just in psychoanalysis and psychotherapy, but everywhere, people construct their relationships in the present by reproducing emotionally important aspects of their past relationships (1, 2).

One way to vividly imagine the impact of transference is to imagine a series of transparent plastic pages in an anatomy text. When the book is first opened, the reader sees the surface of the body. When the first page is turned, the muscles are seen, with the major blood vessels barely visible beneath them. As the reader turns to the next page, the blood vessels and the major nerves are seen. The bones are visible beneath. Finally, when the last page is turned, the bones come into full view. Transference is much the same in that memories of various relationships are superimposed one on another and what we observe on the surface is determined by the subtleties beneath the surface, out of conscious awareness.

Thus, another way of conceptualizing transference is to think of the human mind as made up, in part, of sets of memories of important individuals from a person's past. These organized sets of memories are called *object representations,* and whenever a person meets someone new, he begins to form a new object representation. Obviously, this process proceeds to a significant extent only when the new person is of some importance to the observer;

but whenever that process takes place, the observer, in an effort to understand his or her new acquaintance, scans his memories for standards against which to measure and compare the new individual. Soon, new and old object representations are psychologically connected in response to the observer's need for familiarity and to his other psychological needs (explained below). The newcomer is on the receiving end of ideas, thoughts, and feelings that were originally directed toward the old friend, relative, loved one, or enemy.

What we see when we observe individuals and talk with them about their present life or current relationships is the surface of their psychological life. Beneath that surface are the memories of their important past relationships, which—like the muscles, nerves, and bones beneath the skin—constitute vital parts of the organic whole of their interpersonal world, present as well as past. But the individual perceives his current relationship as the whole. The connections of the current relationship to an old relationship and the way in which the present is serving as a vehicle for working out old relationships remain outside conscious awareness. Therefore, the therapist may experience the transference in the therapy as pressure to behave in a certain way toward the patient that is reminiscent of a previous relationship the patient had in childhood.

■ THE NEED TO REPEAT THE PAST

In all relationships, people form transferences. This is due to our use of the past as a pattern for understanding the present and because there seems to be in all people a psychological need to repeat the past in an effort to master that which was difficult or emotionally painful. Because psychological development invariably involves difficulty and pain, this *compulsion to repeat,* and the transferences that result, are ubiquitous human experiences. In the relationship between a psychoanalyst and a patient in classical psychoanalysis, an unusually intense form of transference—a *transference neurosis*—may develop. In such a situation the analysand has attached to the object representation of the psychoanalyst the important memories, thoughts, feelings, impulses, and conflicts that constitute the core of her emotional disorder. And in the relationship with the analyst the patient will portray the details of this conflict. At the same time the individual will play out in the psychoanalysis other characteristic patterns of interaction with people—patterns that reflect the patient's character structure. This structure, of course, has developed in part in response to the conflicts of childhood.

The entire process happens intensely in psychoanalysis because the patient lies on a couch and does not look at the relatively silent analyst. Both of these techniques decrease the patient's sense of here-and-now reality. In addition, the patient freely associates, thereby bringing unconscious ideas and feelings into consciousness. This process is aided by the analyst's interpretations of the ways the patient blocks the emergence into consciousness of the intense, unconscious transference feelings. In sum, the psychoanalyst supports the activity of the compulsion to repeat. In psychodynamic psychotherapy, the therapist is similarly silent and similarly employs interpretation. This creates an environment in which conscious transference responses are relatively more intense than in typical relationships, although they are less intense than the transference neurosis of psychoanalysis (see Table 8–1).

TABLE 8–1. **Factors influencing the development of the transference**

The patient's need to repeat the past

The psychotherapist's abstinence

Relatively free association by the patient

Interpretation of defenses

Transference interpretations

■ TRANSFERENCE IN PSYCHODYNAMIC PSYCHOTHERAPY

In psychodynamic psychotherapy, the development and under-standing of the transference is one of the therapist's most important tools. It is the vehicle for bringing alive—in the consulting room—the patient's difficulties and for examining these in depth in an existentially meaningful environment. In fact, it is this process that, more than anything else, distinguishes psychodynamic psycho-therapy from other forms.

From another, equally important perspective, the transference is the way the patient remembers what he has forgotten—what is unconscious and the source of psychological pain. In popular caricatures of psychiatric treatment, the patient remembers dra-matic childhood events in a melodramatic fashion. In reality, this remembering occurs as a result of detailed effort to dissect the frequently small memories of long-forgotten, sometimes repeti-tively experienced parts of the past as they present in the transfer-ence relationship. Through the transference the patient develops an understanding of what was experienced in the past and how that experience lives on in the here and now.

Much of a person's mental activity is devoted to keeping that which is outside consciousness unconscious through the use of the person's defense mechanisms or style of thinking. Because the transference usually involves long-forgotten and conflicted parts of relationships, the patient often wants to reject the feelings, thoughts, and memories contained in it, and in the process reject the psychodynamic psychotherapist and flee the therapy. Such resistant transference ideas must be understood if the transference is to be used effectively to bring about a successful outcome to the treatment.

■ FORMS OF TRANSFERENCE

In Chapter 6 the formation of the working or therapeutic alliance was discussed, along with the patient's reaction of frustration that often constitutes the first sign of transference. As the transference develops further, it takes as many forms as there are patients. For each patient-and-therapist team the experience of the transference relationship is unique and demanding. Beginning therapists in particular have usually not previously experienced such strong emotions as love, sexual desire, a sense of frustration to the point of intense dislike or even hatred, insatiable demandingness, or proclamations of total helplessness by individuals who otherwise seem like medical patients coming for a treatment to reduce their pain or to cure their illness.

If the beginning psychiatrist has not previously thought about the contrast between the role of the psychiatrist and other medical specialists, she will at this point. There is no other form of medical treatment in which the physician offers herself as the object of the patient's most intense feelings and allows the patient to experience the physician as the perceived cause of the patient's pain in order to effect a helpful intervention (3). The feelings of the therapist in response to these strong feelings (countertransference) can also be very intense (see Chapter 6).

The psychodynamic psychotherapist must develop confidence in the transference as a therapeutic tool. The beginning therapist often fears that she is harming the patient by helping the patient form a transference. In fact, the therapist is setting the stage for an in-depth exploration of how the patient's mind works and, through that investigation, how the patient can achieve peace of mind.

■ WORKING WITH THE TRANSFERENCE

After the initial transference disappointment is discussed by the patient and psychotherapist and the working alliance has been structured (at least in its initial form), the psychotherapist must be sensitive to the many interactions initiated by the patient. Although these interactions are seemingly matters of business, or of inquiry to facilitate the treatment, the patient will make use of whatever interaction is possible to pattern the present like the past and respond to the compulsion to repeat. The patient forms and plays out the transference reaction with the therapist.

Often, at this point in the treatment, the patient begins to express curiosity about the therapist or complains that the therapist is not doing enough in the face of the patient's overwhelming problems. At other times the patient may express lack of interest in the psychiatrist's efforts in the psychotherapy or may assert that the psychiatrist has accomplished so much that the therapy can be discontinued! Almost any reaction is possible.

Certain rules of thumb will help the psychotherapist work with the transference at this point. The therapist must always wonder what it is the patient is thinking and feeling about the therapist and must not allow himself to think of the patient's comments as neutral remarks about an abstract experience. To help the patient understand transference and begin to develop the ability to work with it, the psychiatrist must direct the patient's attention to this dimension of her thoughts. Thus, the therapist may ask the patient to describe what she thinks or feels about the therapist (4, 5) (Table 8–2). This will focus the attention of both patient and therapist, producing a more detailed picture of the transference, as is seen in the following example:

> A man in his mid-thirties came to treatment during his wife's first pregnancy because of increasing anxiety. After about 6 months, and as his wife neared term, he began to talk about stopping treatment when she delivered. He asserted that the psychiatrist had helped him

---

TABLE 8–2. **Uses of the transference in psychodynamic psychotherapy**

Bring the past alive.

Aid in remembering the past history.

Aid in understanding personal responses in all situations.

---

so much that he could now get on with his life, and he expressed gratitude and praise. Yet the psychiatrist recognized that this man was still troubled by many conflicts. They prevented him from realizing his potential in school, at work, and in his relationships with close friends and loved ones. The psychiatrist also felt that he had conveyed this to his patient. The psychiatrist believed that this talk of stopping, within the transference context, was a resistance—a way of avoiding further therapy—which would uncover the nature of this patient's unconscious impulses and fears.

The psychiatrist took the approach of directing his patient's attention to the transference, with a request: "You say I have helped you a great deal, and you praise me. Tell me some more about how you feel about me at this time. What are your thoughts about me, especially since you know I think there is much work we still have to do together?" The patient responded that he actually felt annoyed at that moment, because he considered the psychiatrist's question intrusive. The psychiatrist asked him to elaborate, again stressing that he was interested in knowing the patient's feelings about him as an intrusive person. In response to that question, put calmly by the psychiatrist, the patient expressed the belief that the psychiatrist wasn't really interested in helping him but in pursuing his own research interests in the therapy. Then the psychiatrist skillfully pointed out that the patient had apparently been reluctant to express this idea before and wondered if there were further problems the patient perceived in the therapeutic approach. This elicited from the patient a long list of complaints about the psychiatrist, accompanied by much previously hidden anger.

Having put all this on the table, without receiving the disapprobation of the psychiatrist, the patient was able to continue therapy, which over the next 2 years focused on his relationship with his overbearing and self-interested father, the memories of whom had been at the root of his early transference reaction.

What is most important about this example is that attention to the transference and to the way in which it was serving as a resistance to further uncovering allowed this patient to move forward in psychotherapy. Had the psychiatrist not been able to tolerate the patient's feelings and explore them in a nonjudgmental atmosphere of safety and neutrality, this treatment would have foundered and been brought to a premature end.

■ TRANSFERENCE AS RESISTANCE

Often patients in psychodynamic psychotherapy are tenacious in their refusal to recognize and explore the transference. They will assert either that their feelings about the therapist are perfectly justified and require no further scrutiny or that they are fleeting and unimportant feelings unworthy of investigation. In either instance the therapist in that situation would do well to describe to the patient a model of transference as a first step in engaging the patient in an exploration of the nature of the transference in her specific case (6–9).

Such a model should include the idea that psychotherapy is a special situation, a kind of stage on which what goes on in the normal course of events is allowed to develop in a more dramatic, and therefore observable, form. But although it is true that what the patient is experiencing, even when it is hardly noticeable, is an exaggeration, the transference situation nonetheless follows the rules of human psychology. We all transfer feelings and ideas from past relationships to present ones. These feelings are very real in a psychological sense. Regardless of what stimulates these feelings, including the real behavior of the therapist, it is useful to look at them in psychotherapy, where they can be used to illuminate the nature of the patient's difficulties. The following illustrates these points:

A very intellectual woman, a physical scientist, came reluctantly for psychodynamic psychotherapy at the insistence of her husband, who found her increasingly distant and emotionally unavailable. She announced to her female psychiatrist at the outset that she did not believe in psychiatry, and she steadfastly rejected all the therapist's efforts to empathize and to understand her plight. The psychotherapist tried to engage her patient in a consideration of what she was feeling toward the therapist, but without success. In response, the patient accused the psychiatrist of badgering her. Indeed, the transference was so intense that there was little chance of developing the necessary therapeutic alliance. The psychiatrist explained the model described above to the patient over a period of several weeks, even while acknowledging that her persistence might be experienced by the patient as a difficult personality trait. Finally, the patient commented that her husband was seen by her as a very persistent individual, as a bully like her father. She had been trying to bully her psychiatrist from day one, experiencing her as though she were an adversary who acted like her husband. From there the patient was able to better use her transference responses as a vehicle for understanding herself, and her treatment progressed.

This case also illustrates the important point that in the transference a therapist of either sex can be connected to a member of the opposite sex (9). Indeed, if a transference is fully understood, it is invariably the case that the psychiatrist is psychologically connected, by the patient, to both parents and is on the receiving end of both loving and aggressive feelings, as is seen in the following example:

A 50-year-old woman came to psychodynamic psychotherapy because of significant difficulty in adjusting to the departure of her adult female children. Near the close of a successful treatment, she told her therapist that she was experiencing the same love for him as she had felt for her mother when she was growing into womanhood. She felt the therapist had helped her come to terms with the demands of another new phase of life, which required her to give up the closest of bonds to her daughters. She remembered that her mother had previously helped the patient give up similar bonds that she had felt toward her mother, when she was about to leave home for college. The psychiatrist did not regard this as a simple statement of affection and appreciation, but rather as an admixture of transference and new feelings. Because his patient had learned to work with transference during the therapy, he noted that, as their work drew to a close, she was feeling toward him as she had toward her mother. He asked if there were other feelings about her mother that came to mind, and she then revealed how angry she had always been at her mother for letting her leave home and how angry she had always been at her father for the same reason. She recalled her anger at her children for leaving her and then her anger at the psychiatrist for allowing their work to draw to a close. This dimension of the patient's anger at both her parents and at her children now came into focus as never before, and through the use of the transference it was understood in depth.

Mastery involved the patient's newly acquired ability to know and accept her anger over separations and the mix in her of angry and loving feelings toward her mother, her father, her children, and anyone, male or female, who ever permitted any separation.

Transference is complex. It crosses gender, it involves feelings experienced originally toward more than one person and individuals of both sexes, and it involves strong positive as well as negative feelings. Further, although transference may be stimulated by what is happening in the here and now, it should be explored for what it is: an opportunity to study the way an individual's past influences her experience of the present.

■ EROTIC AND AGGRESSIVE TRANSFERENCES

When transference is intense, the positive or loving feelings usually involve erotic wishes, and the negative or aggressive feelings involve destructive or hateful wishes. These intense feelings represent the reexperiencing of what the individual first experienced as a child in relation to parents, siblings, and other important individuals during critical phases of psychological development. They are present in the transference because the compulsion to repeat brings them into the relationship with the psychotherapist, although in the majority of cases where they are present, they are, if left unattended, largely unconscious. Thus, these feelings are made conscious by the interventions of the therapist, who has skillfully looked for the patient's mechanisms of thinking that obscure the transference. This permits a detailed and emotionally meaningful exploration of the psychological pain and of the most important factors that have together shaped the patient's personality.

The following example illustrates erotic and aggressive transferences:

A 25-year-old man became depressed and anxious and developed phobic symptoms when faced with the prospect of completing his education and embarking on his career. He entered psychodynamic psychotherapy, and after 6 months he found himself mildly disliking his female psychiatrist. He had a series of dreams that he reported in his sessions. In the dreams he was with various women, all of whom he found unappealing. Yet the psychiatrist noticed that he had begun to come to his sessions very well dressed and groomed and had begun to report how much women liked him and how much they enjoyed him as a sexual partner. The psychiatrist wondered on several occasions whether he was trying to tell her how appealing he would be to her, noting each time how his dress at his sessions had changed. After a number of efforts of this kind, the patient acknowledged that he found her very attractive and had wondered what it would be like to go out with her. There followed over the next 2 years a flowering of a very powerful expression of love and sexual desire for the psychiatrist and fury at her for refusing to date him.

These feelings were connected in the third year of twice-weekly psychodynamic psychotherapy to the patient's realization that as a child he had wanted his mother all for himself and had wished that his father would disappear. His fears of embarking on his career, which had brought him to treatment, were understood as a reluctance to enter the world of adults to compete with grown men for the love of grown women, who unconsciously represented to him his mother. He came to understand that his childhood desire for his mother aroused tremendous anxiety in him.

■ WORKING THROUGH THE TRANSFERENCE

A preoccupation with intense transference feelings can also be used by a patient as a defense to avoid considering the difficulties and conflicts that brought him to therapy. Far more usual, however, in cases where an intense transference develops is the opportunity, over a period of several years, to understand and work through early experiences of fundamental importance to the patient's life. In many disorders, particularly those traditionally called *neuroses* by psychoanalysts, such core experiences involve oedipal feelings of intense love and hatred toward parents. In these cases the transference can bring alive within the consulting room dimly recognized but powerful organizers of thoughts, feelings, and behaviors. The therapist assists the patient in recognizing, understanding, and mastering wishes and impulses that are, when conscious, recognized for what they are: the no longer all-powerful desires of the young child. This process is what is meant by *working through*.

Yet even when the working-through process has taken place, infantile impulses can again find refuge in the unconscious and cause psychic conflict and pain. Thus, successful psychodynamic psychotherapy aims to equip the patient to engage in self-inquiry after the treatment draws to a close in order to ameliorate subsequent psychological difficulty (10). When the transference has flowered and been carefully explored, the probability that the former patient will be successful at maintaining a sense of well-being and mastery is maximized. Also, in the course of the exploration the patient will have mastered many of the skills of self-inquiry, which are further nurtured during the termination phase of treatment.

■ WHEN THERE IS "NO" TRANSFERENCE

Sometimes it may be difficult to identify a transference theme in the relationship with the patient. Transference is a ubiquitous phenomenon, which when identified in therapy will deepen and offer the patient more self-understanding. So how does the clinician respond to the presence of "no" transference?

A good place to start is to remember that "no" transference is itself a transference. The patient is telling the psychiatrist that in the patient's feeling nothing about her there exists a message about his interpersonal life, perhaps as modeled on early relationships. Once the therapist places herself in such a mind set, she can begin to look carefully for signs of transference. Often these come in the form of the therapist's reactions to the patient, especially reactions that do not feel as if they originate in the manifest content of the therapeutic dialogue. An example will help clarify how this works.

A man in his forties came for help because he could not find a woman he wished to marry. Soon, however, he forgot this presenting complaint; yet the treatment continued month after month. When the psychiatrist asked the patient why he continued to come to twice-weekly psychotherapy sessions, where he expressed the feeling he had nothing to say, he answered "because you are the expert, and in the consultation you told me I needed this form of therapy." The therapist then noted that the patient must have feelings about her, since she had advised the treatment and he came for it, but for months had nothing to say. He said only that she was the expert and he welcomed her advice and prized his good fortune in having been referred to her in the first place.

The therapist began to feel uncomfortable with this response, which was repeated whenever she asked her patient how he felt about her or their work together. Eventually, despite her patient's even-tempered and sincere responses, she began to feel goaded and helpless. She wondered whether her patient for some reason wished her to feel this way. As she listened psychodynamically, she heard hints that the patient had always felt teased and goaded by his 4-year-older brother, and eventually she began to inquire more about that relationship. It turned out to be an important one, in which for many years of his childhood the patient had felt helpless and stupid. The therapist wondered next if her countertransference feeling of being goaded and helpless had been a way the patient had communicated to her about this relationship with his brother. This inner musing of the therapist was followed by inquiry aloud, and the patient responded not only that he thought she was right, but that despite his conscious awareness of her kindness, he often felt that she talked down to him and made him feel stupid. Now he realized that this was a transference. For many months the examination of this transference from brother to psychiatrist was the focus of the work. In the end, the patient had a much better understanding of his childhood relationship with his brother and how that reverberated in many of his adult here-and-now relationships.

■ REFERENCES

1. Freud S: The dynamics of transference (1912), in The Standard Edition of the Complete Psychological Works of Sigmund Freud, Vol 12. Translated and edited by Strachey J. London, Hogarth Press, 1958, pp 97–108
2. McLaughlin JT: Transference, psychic reality, and countertransference. Psychoanal Q 50:639–664, 1981
3. Bird B: Notes on transference: universal phenomenon and hardest part of analysis. J Am Psychoanal Assoc 20:267–301, 1972
4. Halpert E: Asclepus: magic in transference to physicians. Psychoanal Q 63:733–755, 1994
5. Ogden TH: Analysing forms of aliveness and deadness of the transference-countertransference. Int J Psychoanal 76:695–709, 1995
6. Brenner C: Psychoanalytic Technique and Psychic Conflict. New York, International Universities Press, 1976
7. Gray P: Psychoanalytic technique and the ego's capacity for viewing intrapsychic activity. J Am Psychoanal Assoc 21:474–494, 1973
8. Loewald HW: On the therapeutic action of psycho-analysis. Int J Psychoanal 41:16–33, 1960
9. Raphling DL, Chused JF: Transference across gender lines. J Am Psychoanal Assoc 36:77–104, 1988
10. Norman HF, Blacker KH, Oremland JD, et al: The fate of the transference neurosis after termination of a satisfactory analysis. J Am Psychoanal Assoc 24:471–498, 1976

■ ADDITIONAL READINGS

Cooper AM: Changes in psychoanalytic ideas: transference interpretation. J Am Psychoanal Assoc 35:77–98, 1987
Freud S: Negation (1925), in The Standard Edition of the Complete Psy-

chological Works of Sigmund Freud, Vol 19. Translated and edited by Strachey J. London, Hogarth Press, 1961, pp 235–239

Sandler J, Dare C, Holder A: The Patient and the Analyst: The Basis of the Psychoanalytic Process. New York, International Universities Press, 1973

9

COUNTERTRANSFERENCE

Countertransference is the emotional reaction of the therapist to the patient. Historically, countertransference was limited in meaning to the therapist's transference onto the patient. This was felt to be a response to the patient's transference. Like all transferences, the therapist's countertransference was the result of unconscious conflicts; however, these unresolved conflicts were those of the therapist rather than those of the patient. This countertransference was thought to obscure the therapist's judgment in conducting the therapy.

Countertransferences are many and varied. Often they are the result of events occurring in the therapist's life that may make him more sensitive to certain themes in the patient's associations. The developmental period of the therapist's life—involving issues of intimacy, achievement, or old age, for example—may also affect how the therapist hears the patient. Intense transferences of all kinds—erotic, aggressive, devaluing, idealizing, and others—are ripe for serving as the stimulus to awaken in the therapist elements of his own past. The psychiatrist in training may feel the push and pull of the demands of training, the workload, or the beginnings and endings of rotations and may find "all" his patients talking about the same theme, which just "happens" to match the therapist's concerns. When all one's patients seem to be talking about feeling overworked or angry or sad, the therapist can reflect on these feelings and wonder whether this theme is being selected by him rather than being the central issue for all his patients. Finally, a common countertransference issue in training occurs at the end of training when both the therapist and the patient are dealing with termination. For the patient it is the end of treatment; for the therapist it is both the end of a treatment and the end of a stage of life, usually accompanied by a move and loss of colleagues and friends as well as a sense of new achievement. This complex emotional interplay can lead to the patient's experience of the ending being overlooked, as in the following example:

> The young therapist was preparing to complete training and move to a new city with a feeling of sadness and also great accomplishment. The patient was planning to begin a new marriage. The therapist became concerned that the patient was making a bad choice and was acting impulsively. He was concerned that something would happen that would "injure" the patient's life. The therapist sought out and discussed his feelings with a colleague. The colleague listened and said that it sounded as if the patient was making a reasonable decision and that the patient was talking about how the therapy had helped him and would be missed. That night the therapist had a dream in which it was snowing in the month of July. He thought about the dream and recalled a vague memory of a separation from his father. The separation was in December, and the therapist—then 3 years old—was in danger from a serious illness. The patient came to mind, and the therapist realized he was seeing his anxiety about the separation and about "leaving father behind" in his view of the patient. The therapist felt much relief from his overconcern for the patient and was better able to hear the patient's feelings of success and hope and to experience his own.
>
> In this case, the therapist had begun to see in the patient his own concerns and fears and was defending against the feelings of pride and accomplishment he felt

in his achievements. His listening to the patient had as a result become distorted both by hearing a wrong emphasis (i.e., anxiety) and by missing an important theme (i.e., accomplishment, competition, and success). The therapist appropriately sought a colleague's ear to aid in processing the countertransference feelings.

More recently, the term *countertransference* has been increasingly used to describe nearly all the emotional reactions of the therapist to the patient in the therapeutic setting. Such reactions may be either a potential block or a potential aid to understanding—a tool for better understanding the patient. The clinician may first note a patient's core conflictual issue through observing subtle emotional reactions stirred in herself. The clinician can then explore these feelings, through self-analysis, as possible reverberations from the unconscious but also as emerging concerns of the patient that may be hidden in the patient's language, behavior, or fantasies, as in the following example:

An isolated, middle-aged schoolteacher spoke in a stilted and distant voice about her criticisms of her co-workers and then about the many inadequacies of her therapist. "I don't want to talk to you," she said. "I feel you are very far away and not paying any attention." In response, the therapist felt distant, bored, stung by the criticism, and defensive about his work. Shortly thereafter, the patient associated her feelings to her emotional distance from family members. She felt unloved, unappreciated, and criticized, especially by her mother. She described having withdrawn, as a result, into a lifelong emotional isolation; she despaired of ever loving and valuing herself enough to find a loving, warm, intimate relationship. The therapist thought of how the patient had adopted her mother's hypercritical and emotionally distant posture to defend against her longings to be valued and admired. Now, seeing this, the therapist recognized his own hurt feelings and withdrawal as a pale version of the patient's chronic sense of hurt and way of coping by distancing.

The countertransference, as in this vignette, can provide an opportunity. Beginning therapists are especially vulnerable to the devaluing of themselves done by a hostile patient. Facing their own concerns about competence, fears of a supervisor's criticism, and anxiety about learning a new skill, beginning therapists can feel swept up by a patient's accusations about their inexperience or inadequacy. Patients frequently hurt their therapists' feelings, bore them, and offend them in various ways. Lingering too long over the seeming truth of a patient's emotional reactions toward the therapist, either positive or negative, can distract attention from the important omnipresent fact of the transference. In the preceding vignette the therapist did feel bored, unavailable, and defensive. But the silver lining to this particular emotional cloud was the therapist's ability to recognize his experience as an echo of the lifelong emotional position of his patient. Devastated by criticism and feeling devalued, unloved, and unlovable, the patient had withdrawn in childhood into an aloof and hypercritical stance to hide and protect her hurt feelings and longings for closeness. The psychodynamic psychotherapist observes his own emotional reactions and values, and he processes them as possible windows on the patient's experience. Frequently, the more intense and even embarrassing the therapist's responses, the more likely they are to reflect a crucial, hidden, conflicted state residing within the patient.

■ CONCORDANT AND COMPLEMENTARY COUNTERTRANSFERENCES

There are two types of countertransference reactions: concordant and complementary (1). These reactions correspond to an identification with the emotional position of the patient or to an identification with a person from the patient's past (usually a parent) (Table 9–1). In the clinical vignette described above, the hurt, devalued position evoked in the therapist was a concordant countertransference—the therapist was experiencing empathy with the patient's usual emotional position. If the therapist had resisted the painful, devalued concordant identification and had fought back with a reactive criticalness and hostility in self-defense, he would have been evidencing a complementary countertransference—taking the position of an important figure from the patient's past. In that case, the clinician would have been taking the part of the critical mother, now internalized as part of the patient's overly harsh conscience.

A great deal of emotional power lies in the countertransference. Enacting a complementary countertransference can undermine a benevolently neutral therapeutic position, leading to a repetition in the treatment rather than a helpful reworking of the infantile conflicts. Conversely, using the countertransference to shape and inform interpretations can be among the most powerful of therapeutic tools, as is shown in the following example:

> Months later in treatment, the inhibited and emotionally distant schoolteacher described in the previous section defended bitterly and sadly her firm conviction that she could never marry. All men were dominating and abusive, she maintained. In fact, in all her affairs she had been disappointed and exploited. With an enormous struggle, she then confided to the therapist her lifelong

TABLE 9–1. **Types of countertransference reactions**

Concordant: The therapist experiences and empathizes with the patient's emotional position.
Complementary: The therapist experiences and empathizes with the feelings of an important person from the patient's life.

sexual fantasy that involved being abused by a domineering and hypercritical man. The therapist then pointed out the patient's self-fulfilling prophecy. Preoccupied with a sadomasochistic sexual idea, the patient had unconsciously sought men who would entice and then betray her, a scenario that had been repeated numerous times. The patient flew into a sudden rage, attacking the therapist for his "denigrating" interpretation. The therapist felt stung by the ferocity of her attack. He felt angry, defensive, and also vaguely guilty that perhaps his intervention had not been tactful and had also constituted a disrespectful attack. The therapist contained his reaction and thought about it silently. He was then able to say that he appreciated how difficult it was for the patient to be explicit about her sexual longings, and that perhaps, out of her great sensitivity, the patient had experienced the therapist as yet another enticing but contemptuous man who invited an intimacy but then abused her. The patient agreed with this formulation and also then concurred with the first interpretation that had so enraged her.

The patient had clung to the depressing idea that all men were abusive because it was even more painful to admit how her own fantasy life had shaped the string of degrading affairs. The therapist had thought to himself how his first interpretation had been constructed both from empathic constructive impulses to inform and liberate and from irritation with the patient's grim depression, defeatism, and stubbornly bleak vision of humanity. Dwelling too guiltily on his own aggression would have been a trap for the therapist and would have blocked the way in which the conflict had become alive in psychotherapy. The therapist had experienced both complementary and concordant countertransferences. Identifying with the patient's experience of depression, helplessness, and frustration was the concordant posi-

tion. His irritation at (and rejection of) the patient's
angry, bitter, hurt position was an identification with the
critical and contemptuous internalized parents from the
patient's past. Tolerating and processing both aspects led to
a helpful interpretation of a highly charged transference-
countertransference situation.

Patients invariably defeat their therapists in both subtle and
obvious ways. It is one way they let therapists know how they are
stymied by the defeats in their own lives that have brought them
into treatment. Defeating a therapist's best efforts is also a way of
expressing competitiveness toward the therapist, who is seen with
envy as being more powerful and less troubled. A young therapist's
need to please the supervisor and to counteract her own anxious or
guilty sense of inexperience is at odds with the patient's need to
stump and defeat the therapist.

Very sick, hostile, and attacking patients can damage their
therapist's self-esteem, which leads to countertransference hatred
(2). Usually this hatred is covered by boredom or withdrawal in
the therapist and by a covert wish that the patient would interrupt
therapy. With borderline, psychotic, and suicidal patients, this
secret wish by the therapist can, in fact, exacerbate a patient's
suicidal potential, because it constitutes an attitude of rejection and
abandonment.

Experienced clinicians learn to adopt a position of humility and
attenuated therapeutic zeal that protects against this particularly
dangerous transference-countertransference situation. An attitude
of concern, sprinkled with the recognition that the most skilled of
clinicians can never fully control therapeutic success, can go a long
way toward shielding the therapist from the common transferential
attack, "If my treatment is a failure, it proves that you, the therapist,
are a failure." Withstanding this kind of pressure on one's professional self-esteem is easier for an experienced clinician with a
history of successfully conducted treatment cases. It is helpful for

a young therapist to keep in mind that this kind of transference is extremely common and is not to be taken at face value. Every therapist will hear it time and again throughout her career, often from patients who eventually do very well in treatment.

Containing and processing countertransference necessarily involves a split in the functioning of the therapist. The therapist develops both a reacting, feeling half and an honestly self-observing and formulating half that works to understand countertransference feelings with an eye to forming useful interpretations. It is very important for a therapist to notice and contain irritation that occurs in response to the patient's provocation. It is also crucial to avoid responding while under the sway of such angry feelings. Patients usually pick up a therapist's affect from her tone of voice. An accurate but angrily delivered interpretation can be felt as a repetition of earlier trauma instead of a helpful intervention.

Conscious effort to look for both the concordant and the complementary countertransferences is an important technique to master. When, in the heat of the transference, a patient casts the therapist in the role of villain, similar to the past villains from the patient's life, the therapist will generally struggle with the complementary countertransference. The therapist needs then to search for the concordant set of feelings in order to grope her way back to the patient's usual emotional position. Often it is this part of the patient that is feeling attacked by the patient's own internalized demons, which have been cast upon the therapist.

A brilliant and accomplished schizoid woman patient complained softly, "I resent coming two times a week and paying for missed appointments while I'm out of town. I'm thinking of cutting back here or of looking for a different kind of therapy. I came here some time ago because I had never had an intimate relationship and it seems that I still can't." In a low tone of voice she also complained that the therapist was exploitative, quite possibly dishonest, and definitely arrogant, since she always remained calm in the face of the patient's dissatisfaction. The therapist felt a wave of intense outrage at the blanket assault on her skills and her ethics. However, she processed her reaction as reminiscent of the patient's description of how she often felt after letters, phone calls, and visits from her mother. Her mother had frequently criticized every aspect of the patient: dress, posture, hair color, figure, friends, apartment, and lifestyle. Using this thought, the therapist commented about the patient's many past experiences of feeling devalued and wondered if the patient was aware of how angry she felt, since she expressed her anger in such an indirect way, with a low, offhand tone of voice. Intrigued, the patient agreed that she often did not admit to herself how angry she really was. Consciously, she experienced herself as helpless and exploited. The therapist was able to use this intervention to develop a picture of the patient's experience in her family and of how the family must have handled aggression.

In this example, the therapist, cast as an exploitative villain, felt an intense hostility in a complementary countertransference. She was able to contain and process the feelings and find her way back into the more concordant position of identifying with the patient's dilemma (Table 9–2).

As in the above example, it is always important first to understand and dissolve negative countertransference before attempting to interpret and dissolve the negative transference. In explaining a patient's hostility, the therapist has to feel his or her way into the patient's position to understand and articulate what provokes it. Merely pointing out a patient's aggressiveness, out of context, is generally experienced by the patient as an unhelpful criticism or attack.

TABLE 9–2.   **Processing the countertransference**

The therapist should

Be alert to his or her own developmental and life issues.

Not take the patient's feelings personally.

Not enact the countertransference.

Use the countertransference to help form interpretations.

Use countertransference anger to understand the patient's hostility.

Examine his or her own emotional reactions for clues to the patient's dynamics.

With borderline patients, diagnose split-apart self and object images by linking transference and countertransference.

Search for the concordant countertransference when experiencing the complementary countertransference.

■ COUNTERTRANSFERENCE IN WORK WITH BORDERLINE PERSONALITY DISORDER PATIENTS

Countertransference emerges in typical patterns in certain diagnostic categories. As a group, patients with borderline personality disorder have poorly integrated their loving and hostile feelings, both toward themselves and toward the important people in their lives. Typically, in the course of dynamic psychotherapy, borderline patients will express positively and negatively toned images of themselves and others in their lives. Frequently these images are seemingly expressed separately and sequentially, rather than as a whole set of feelings complexly mixed and ambivalently felt. The therapist's countertransference feelings may then constitute a bewilderingly disconnected sequence of emotional reactions (3). These feelings are the result of the patient's unintegrated and widely disparate moods, self-presentations, and modes of relating to the therapist, as seen in the following example:

A borderline patient complained for many sessions of her emotional isolation, depression, sexual inhibition, and deprivation. A product of a rigid and puritanically religious home, the patient had absorbed a harsh conscience, full of fire and brimstone and her mother's sternly religious prohibitions. After many sessions of describing her fear of her mother's criticism, the patient presented a dream in which her mother stood on a table with an accusing finger pointed at the patient, who was cowering below. In the very next session the patient demanded that her therapist explain her symptoms to her. She insisted that after seeing her all these months, the therapist should have a complete understanding of her case. Treatment was taking too long. She suspected that other forms of therapy were better and faster. The therapist first experienced a rush of guilt because she was unable to present a formulation of the patient's case. The therapist wished that she could do it on the spot to appease her angry patient! It then suddenly occurred to the clinician that she was now in the patient's usual position—as in the dream—"cowering under the table." The patient had enacted the image of the demanding, intimidating mother.

As seen in this case, this borderline patient enacted different pieces of her important relationships at different times. One day she was the small, guilty child; the next day she was the demanding and intimidating mother, assigning the little-girl image of herself, with all her frightened feelings, to her therapist. The sequentially expressed, unintegrated pieces of the transference and of the resulting countertransference were then available for the therapist to integrate in her own mind to present back to the patient. With this type of patient, the therapist must think across time and from one feeling state to another to process the countertransference. The feelings aroused in the therapist may be quite disparate and separated in time and yet must be recalled and remembered to understand the patient's psychic reality.

■ OTHER COUNTERTRANSFERENCES

There are, of course, many other types of countertransference reactions besides irritation and defensiveness. Boredom in the therapist is usually a countertransference sign that a patient is dealing with heavily conflicted and heavily defended feelings and impulses, frequently of rage. Feelings of protectiveness toward a patient can signal a genuine emotional fragility in the patient, necessitating caution and tact, but they can also be a part of an unconscious transference-countertransference collusion to avoid areas of conflict in the patient that should be addressed. The therapist who takes things personally and concretely in the here and now can fall into a countertransference trap that abrogates his role and his therapeutic contract to explore the origins and dynamics of the patient's conflicts.

Narcissistic patients often idealize their therapists to a superhuman degree. Their therapists need both to tolerate the exaggerated admiration without too much embarrassment and to avoid basking in it with too much pleasure. Either approach would prevent exploration and confrontation in the treatment. Erotic transferences that stimulate eroticized countertransferences are often among the most difficult for beginning therapists to contain and process. Frequently the therapist may feel embarrassed and unable to describe the erotic feelings to a supervisor and may not recognize how these feelings can be an avenue to understanding either an emerging sexual (often oedipal) or a defended aggressive theme. Often the highly erotic transference and countertransference are not recognized as an idealization of the therapist that contains few truly sexual feelings. The erotic feelings are an expression of the patient's feelings of omnipotence and his hope for and fear of separation and aggression in the therapeutic relationship. As always, these reactions need to be tolerated with honesty and respect for the valuable information being communicated about the patient's conflicts and early life, all of which is therapeutic gold to be mined interpretively. The therapist's increasing ability to use the countertransference is a sign of increasing therapeutic skill.

■ THE THERAPIST'S NEED FOR PERSONAL PSYCHOANALYSIS AND SUPERVISION

Along with its rewards, psychodynamic psychotherapy is highly demanding work, stirring in the psychotherapist her own unconscious and conscious wishes, fears, and conflicts. Simply put, it is not really possible to do this kind of work well without a deep understanding of oneself. Freud (4) recognized this, specifically enjoining those who came after him to have not only a training psychoanalysis but subsequent periodic psychoanalysis. He also prescribed the practice of self-analysis. He advised this because he felt that dealing in psychotherapy with the unconscious processes of one's patients causes resonances and reverberations in one's own unconscious, which, if not recognized and understood, could impair the psychiatrist's ability to work effectively. Today these injunctions are often ignored, but not without consequence.

Personal therapy or psychoanalysis, particularly while the therapist is engaged in psychotherapeutic work, can greatly aid the therapist's development of skill in recognizing and using the countertransference. There are, of course, psychiatrists who choose to do very little psychodynamic psychotherapy but who nonetheless want to carry a small but steady caseload of such patients. For these clinicians, the investment in personal psychoanalysis, or even personal psychodynamic psychotherapy, may seem out of proportion to their efforts in this area. Although there is no substitute for such self-understanding, an alternate possibility is supervision on a regular basis with a specialist in psychoanalysis or psychodynamic psychotherapy. Indeed, in that setting the psychiatrist may learn of ongoing countertransference difficulties and can then undertake personal treatment. On the other hand, regular supervision may prove sufficient.

■ REFERENCES

1. Racker H: Transference and Countertransference. New York, International Universities Press, 1968
2. Buie D, Maltsberger JT: Countertransference hate in the treatment of suicidal patients. Arch Gen Psychiatry 30:625–633, 1974
3. Kernberg OF: Transference and countertransference in the treatment of borderline patients, in Object-Relations Theory and Clinical Psychoanalysis. New York, Jason Aronson, 1976, pp 161–184
4. Freud S: Analysis terminable and interminable (1937), in The Standard Edition of the Complete Psychological Works of Sigmund Freud, Vol 23. Translated and edited by Strachey J. London, Hogarth Press, 1964, pp 209–253

■ ADDITIONAL READINGS

Gabbard GO, Wilkinson SM: Management of Countertransference With Borderline Patients. Washington, DC, American Psychiatric Press, 1994

Giovacchini P: Countertransference Triumphs and Catastrophes. Northvale, NJ, Jason Aronson, 1989

Maroda K: The Power of Counter-transference: Innovations in Analytic Technique. Northvale, NJ, Jason Aronson, 1991

Searles HF: Countertransference and Related Subjects. New York, International Universities Press, 1979

Tower L: Countertransference. J Am Psychoanal Assoc 4:224–255, 1956

10

DREAMS

Freud called the psychoanalysis of dreams the "royal road to the unconscious" (1, p. 100). The clinical use of dreams in dynamic psychotherapy offers the psychiatrist many opportunities to assist the patient in developing an understanding of how the mind works (Table 10–1). Dreams also allow the practitioner to develop a detailed understanding of the typical ways a patient thinks, feels, defends, and resists (1–4). They provide a window through which one can glimpse unconscious ideas and memories that are of central importance to the patient's life experience (5). Dream analysis can also be an important vehicle to help the patient develop skills in ongoing self-inquiry (6).

■ THE USE OF DREAMS IN PSYCHOTHERAPY

Introducing the Patient to the Use of Dreams

Early in treatment, before defenses are heightened in response to the initial probing, dreams may be very revealing of the patient's central problems and conflicts (7). In the opening phase, dream interpretations should focus on the surface of the dreamer's experience—the manifest content, as revealed in the actual dream hallucination (Table 10–2). Indeed, throughout the opening phase of treatment and beyond, the psychodynamic psychotherapist emphasizes the patient's recent experience more than the past; this is also true with dreams. The therapist focuses more on the dream's

TABLE 10–1.	Goals for the use of dreams in psychotherapy

Clarify defense mechanisms and resistances.

Help define and illustrate the transference.

Make conscious the patient's unconscious dynamics, conflicts, and memories.

Aid in learning ongoing self-inquiry.

TABLE 10–2.	Techniques for using dreams in psychotherapy

Early in therapy:

Focus on the day residue and the manifest content.

Identify and illustrate defense mechanisms and resistances in the dream.

Focus on transference manifestations in the dream.

Later in therapy:

Use the dream to indicate the unconscious wishes, fears, and conflicts.

day residue—the recent parts of the patient's life that serve as the source of material for constructing the dream.

This focus establishes for the patient the fact that dreams are connected to waking, real-life experiences. The patient learns that dreams can be examined and understood; this initial understanding in turn prepares the patient for the deeper and more unconscious meanings of the dream, reflecting childhood wishes and fears. In this way, the secret, underlying concerns that trouble the patient and that are expressed in his dreams can be slowly revealed, examined, understood, and mastered as the patient is able to discover these layers of meaning (5). In this manner, dreams also become a model of mental functioning for the patient to "play with" and understand.

For example, a young, single, female physician-in-training had enjoyed great success and happiness until she began her first year of postgraduate training. She experienced increasing anxiety when she was required to care for critically ill patients. She experienced herself as being inadequate to the task and possessing too little knowledge to do her job successfully, despite an outstanding academic record and a well-documented fund of information. For these reasons she had begun twice-weekly psychotherapy 6 months earlier.

One day she was assigned to care for a patient with a virulent infectious disease, who, despite vigorous efforts, died. The attending physician on the case, and other more experienced house officers who had worked with the physician-in-training, reassured her that her efforts had been well directed. But, as was typical for her, in her own mind she felt that she had failed her patient. That night, exhausted, she fell deeply asleep and dreamed that she was alone in a strange place, a city where she recognized no one and where nothing was familiar. She felt bewildered. Then a feeling of shame came over her, because she felt she should have been able to orient herself and find her own way. She noticed that she was near a train station, so she decided to go inside and get information about where she was. She thought she could find a bookstore and buy a guidebook. She figured she would decide how to proceed after that. She then felt better in the dream.

The next day she began her psychotherapy session by describing her feeling that she had failed her patient. Soon, she remembered her dream and reported it as related above. Her psychiatrist, acutely aware that his patient had hardly worked with dreams in the course of her therapy, responded by first asking her what she thought about the dream. The patient said that it reminded her of how she had felt the previous day in response to the death of her patient. The psychiatrist asked how this was so, and the patient said that she had felt bewildered when so sick a patient had come to her ward and had felt ashamed of this feeling. The psychiatrist commented that it appeared that she had dreamed what she did in response to these feelings. He also indicated that the dream appeared to resolve the difficult feelings in a particular way: she tried to read her way out of it. She responded that studying and reading had stood her in good stead all her life, for she was a doctor because she had always been a dedicated student. From there the session continued with a discussion of her experience in medical school, which she had enjoyed.

Use of Dreams During the Middle Phase of Therapy

In the case being discussed, about 6 months later, the physician-in-training discussed above had a similar experience of confusion and shame in response to the demands of a critically ill patient, and she again reported the identical dream. This time the psychiatrist had a better understanding of his patient. He now knew that the patient felt conflict over the active (visible for others to see) use of her skills, especially when these skills drew attention to her. Her preferred style was to be retiring and thoughtful. So this time, when they discussed the dream, the psychiatrist noted that she, as the maker of the dream—the scriptwriter, so to speak—had depicted herself as lost and confused and looking for a bookstore when there might have been other alternatives. He wondered what advantage there was to her in casting herself in such a role. By this time the patient knew something of her mechanisms of defense and resistance. She responded that she did not like to think of herself as being active, or competent, which seemed too showy and made her the center of attention. The nature of her characterological defense mechanism, being quiet, thoughtful, and inactive, so central to her personality, was crystallized by the dream. Thus summarized and illustrated, the dream could serve as a shorthand for the focus of the work. In fact, it remained the focus of her therapy for the next several months.

Use of Dreams During the Latter Phases of Therapy

One year later in the psychotherapy discussed above, much time had been devoted to the physician-in-training's preference for avoiding being the center of attention, particularly when she worked with her male colleagues. This preference had also become clear in her transference to her male psychiatrist. In her social life she tended to be shy and retiring, though she often dated. Nevertheless, she always felt dissatisfied with the way she related to her male friends, because she felt she was unable to enjoy herself in a zestful, passionate way.

This time, when she had a similar experience with one of her patients, and reported the same dream, the therapist chose to ask her associations to the dream. Indeed, he had been doing this with most dreams she reported during the second year of their work together, and this time he did it with this now repetitive dream. He asked her what her thoughts were about each aspect of the dream—for example, wondering what came to her mind when she pictured the strange city, or the railroad station, in her mind's eye or thought about the imagined bookstore. It was then that new information came out about the patient's past that she felt was important to understanding who she was and how she came to be the way she was. When asked about the railroad station, she associated this element of the dream with going to the railroad station every summer, from the age of 7 on, to travel to the country to attend summer camp. She remembered that at those times her mother was always very tearful. She added that she had not thought about that for many years.

Spurred on by this recovered memory, she spoke about her relationship with her mother in a way she never had before. Her mother had been a retiring sort herself and had encouraged the patient to study hard to become a scholar. But her mother had found it difficult when her daughter, the patient, had blossomed into such an active and aggressive youngster. Her mother never expected her to win a college scholarship and leave home. Although her mother had mouthed her approval, her sadness over losing her child had also been communicated. The patient recalled finding this extremely difficult. Indeed, in response to her mother's covert messages that she remain close by, the patient had felt throughout childhood a conflict over separating from her mother. The patient then noticed that in the repetitive dream, she, the dreammaker, had chosen not to create a male character, a handsome stranger whom she might have boldly and zestfully approached for directions and with whom she might then have spent her day. She also noted that this same shyness had always held her back in talking with her male psychiatrist.

By working with her dreams, this patient had learned to tap her capacity for imagination and to more freely associate. She gained a sense of what she really wanted and of what wishes were struggling to come into consciousness. Over the next year the patient came to appreciate that her sense of confusion and shame in clinical situations was derived from her feelings about her mother, as was her conflict over being active, aggressive, and ultimately very appealing to men, including her male psychiatrist.

In this case the repetitive dream illustrates the way early dream material may include clues to the central dynamics of a person's personality and the ways dream material can be used as psychodynamic psychotherapy progresses. The use of the manifest content and day residue, the subsequent opportunity to understand transference and defense mechanisms, and, eventually, the opportunity to probe unconscious wishes, fears, and conflicts unfold as the psychotherapy deepens (Table 10–2). Certainly, in this case, work with dreams served as an organizer of this patient's psychotherapy—a place where new ideas were generated and from which new perspectives emerged to be applied in other ways in her therapy. Like any example, it is chosen because it is unusually clear, for in most cases dreams occur in a more random fashion, work with them is less systematic, and the resulting understanding is less dramatic. Nevertheless, it does serve to indicate the possibilities for gaining understanding of a patient through the use of dreams in psychodynamic psychotherapy.

■ THE DREAM AS AN INDICATOR OF UNCONSCIOUS CONFLICT

Another characteristic of dreams in psychodynamic psychotherapy is that they may, after becoming more obscure as defenses are initially mobilized, become clearer as defenses and resistances are understood and abandoned. Should this occur, the therapist will be able to use dreams as guideposts in defining core unconscious desires and conflicts as they emerge into consciousness, as is shown in the following example:

A male patient in his early thirties was in his third year of psychodynamic psychotherapy. He had become aware that his need to compete with male authority figures reflected feelings of competition with his father for the attention of his mother. This understanding was accompanied by increased dating, which was particularly significant, because his initial complaint had involved general feelings of social inhibition, particularly shyness with women. One night, after a date that included sexual intercourse with a woman he particularly liked, he dreamed that he was going to a costume ball with his male therapist and that they were both dressed in kilts, appearing to be robust Scotsmen.

The therapist asked for his associations to each of the two figures as they appeared in the dream. The patient responded that the dream did not surprise him, at least in part, because his psychiatrist was a Scotsman! Then, as he pondered the dream images, he spoke of how he viewed his therapist as powerful, as the very model of a strong man, and he noted that he would sometimes daydream of how he wished to be like his therapist. He associated these feelings to how he used to think of his father in the same way. The patient then noted that he himself was different. Although the kilt may have been manly when worn by a man, his kilt was a sign that he was quite feminine, at least when he thought about wearing one. Then he spoke of how, whenever he thought of himself and his father, initial similarities always switched to differences, for he thought of himself as weak and his father as strong. He observed that thinking of himself as less than a strong man was a common way in which he had always avoided heterosexual social opportunities, especially at times when he felt strong, powerful, and sexually attractive. He commented that perhaps there was a connection between his guilt over his feelings about his mother and his need to avoid situations where he could have sex with women.

In this case a dream opened up a new layer of the unconscious conflict. The patient used his understanding of the dream to shed light both on present conflicts and on past patterns of behavior. The clarity of this patient's dream, with its clearly sexual overtones, indicates the low level of defense operative at that time in the treatment and therefore the availability of unconscious material that was usually well defended. The therapist must be alert to not go too deep when the material is so very rich. The depth of discussion should match where the treatment is in all its elements, not just the occurrence of one dream. Similarly, a clear dream should not be avoided, for it is one way in which the patient is indicating a readiness to approach a new topic.

■ THE DREAM AS AN INDICATOR OF TRANSFERENCE

Dreams can be important in illustrating the nature of the transference at any point in psychodynamic psychotherapy. Whether the transference is characterized by feelings of love or hate, affection or rage, boredom or excitement, sexual desire or the wish to flee, or a spirit of cooperation or opposition, attention to and interpretation of dreams can bring the transference into perspective (8). The following two examples are presented to clarify the clinical technique of handling dreams in the course of psychodynamic psychotherapy. The reader should review the discussion of dreams in the sections on beginning treatment (Chapter 6) and the opening phase (see above) for the special handling of dreams at those times.

> *Case 1.* During the first year of treatment, a middle-aged woman complained often that her psychotherapy was not helping her. She reported a dream in which she was a small child in school. In the afternoon she and her classmates went to play on the school field, and while they were playing, the sky suddenly turned very dark. Off in the distance she saw her teacher waving to the

group of students with whom she played. But the patient could not figure out what the teacher was trying to communicate.

After eliciting the day residue, the patient's psychiatrist asked the patient to describe what came into her mind as she thought about each scene in the dream. The patient noted that in the dream she could not understand what her teacher was trying to communicate, and added that, although she had been reluctant to say so, she felt the same way about her psychiatrist's efforts at communication. There ensued a discussion of the relationship between the psychiatrist and the patient, centering on the patient's feeling that her therapist neither understood nor was able to talk with her. This led to a renewed effort by the psychiatrist to understand the patient's worries about being understood, and the therapy then moved forward.

Case 2. A depressed, anxious patient in his forties dreamed of being chased by a group of soldiers, who slashed at him with their bayonets. He hid under a table, and several hours later he came out of hiding and escaped. The psychiatrist asked the patient to say what came to mind as he thought of each scene or component in the dream. The patient thought about the table and noted that it was similar to the one next to his psychiatrist's chair. When thinking about the soldiers and their bayonets, he associated these thoughts with the psychiatrist, who, he noted, often used a pipe tool to clean his pipe, which he smoked during therapy sessions. The psychiatrist asked if the patient felt as though he were on the receiving end of slashing comments, from which he had to hide during his therapy hours, and there ensued a discussion that corroborated this feeling. The patient then recalled historical experiences with his parents that were the basis of the transference feeling. Over the next several weeks the patient began to tell his therapist more openly when he felt hurt. Thereafter, they were able to understand the significance of those times to the patient and to understand what past memories were active when the patient felt that way.

These cases involve patients who have learned what a dream is and how to use dreams to deepen their understanding of their experiential world. When the patient has developed this ability to use the components of a dream as a jumping-off point for relatively free association, much can be learned, particularly about the transference. This can greatly enhance the patient's understanding of personal internal conflicts.

■ THE DREAM AS INDICATOR OF GENETIC DATA OR ADAPTATIONAL STYLE

Today, much is made of the recovery of false memories in psychotherapy. Psychiatrists skilled in psychodynamic psychotherapy do sometimes find in a patient's dreams clues about forgotten experiences that were developmentally important as organizers of personality structure. Such clues must always be verified by other data, because recall in psychotherapy—in particular, in dreams—does not ensure that such memories are true rather than later reconstructions, screen memories, or wished-for events. Similarly, dreams may provide clues about how a patient has developed a style of adaptation and why that person did so:

A tenured professor in his fifties was in twice-weekly psychodynamic psychotherapy because he was not satisfied with his scholarly productivity. He began to dream about reading, night after night. Sometimes he was reading at his desk in his home, sometimes he was again a graduate student working on his dissertation, and sometimes he was a child in the early years of elementary school, enjoying the first flush of his intellectual power as he read childhood classics. He continued to dream. His associations to the dreams shifted, and he always ended up unhappy, for reasons he could not fathom. As the psychiatrist inquired about his associations to being unhappy, the patient noted that he loved reading and study, even though from an early age it had set him apart from his peers. He had looked forward to going to a special high school, where he would be with other gifted students, and in his memory that had worked out well indeed. By the time he arrived at a fine university, he was a confirmed scholar, happy to be in a place where he would train to be a professor and meet others similarly inclined.

At that point he remembered wistfully how he had felt when his younger sister arrived at the same university. She was a beautiful young woman, very social and not so single-mindedly dedicated to her studies. She had teased him about being a bookworm, but always affectionately, and he recalled his loving feelings toward her. Then, suddenly, during a discussion about his sister, he began to cry. He recalled how she had died 25 years earlier in an accident and how in response he had retreated even more passionately into his studies. His psychiatrist noted all this, and he felt that he was hearing important material, but he could not yet put it together.

Next the patient wondered why he was thinking about his sister, because, although he had loved her, he believed that he had gotten over her death and really had not spoken or thought much about her for the last 10 years. He associated to his own mother, who had been encouraging, loving, yet reserved in a sense about his early commitment to a scholarly life. After all, she would say, "There's more to life than reading . . . there's being with people . . . books will always be there, people will not." As he remembered this, he began to cry, again noting he had not thought about his mother's wisdom in many years. Indeed, over the next few sessions he brought in letters from his mother and a journal he had kept, which corroborated his recollection that they had discussed this subject often.

This patient was a sensitive man, possessed of both a passion for learning and a passion for living. But throughout his life, when inevitable choices had to be made, he chose his intellect, which allowed him to advance educationally and professionally. It had seemed to him a safer journey to navigate, a course more under his control. His sister's accidental death had for him represented a confirmation of this view.

Next, this patient asked himself why at this time he had become unproductive, why he had sought therapy, and why he had dreamed so much about reading, with associated feelings of unhappiness. He realized then that his two children were about to leave home for university. His children were high achievers, and he was very proud of them. They were part of a loving family, which included the patient's wife, their mother. Yet beneath this picture-book situation were doubts within the professor's mind: he wondered whether they had all spent too little time just enjoying each other, too much time reading and studying.

At this point. the patient was well understood by his therapist and himself. Together they were able to consider his conflict over his priorities, and they understood the symptom he had developed: dissatisfaction with his scholarly productivity. The result of this psychodynamic inquiry was not dramatic, but it was profound. The professor felt better about his work and better about his family. When he was in conflict, he could recognize consciously what was going on in his mind and self-consciously decide what he most desired and would enjoy—time with a book or time with his family. Consideration of his dreams had been the focal point for this successful therapeutic intervention.

■ THE TERMINATION DREAM

At the end of psychodynamic psychotherapy, another dream phenomenon is sometimes observed: the termination dream. Such a dream will often awaken in the psychiatrist, the patient, or both an awareness that termination may be in order. In such a dream the patient experiences her problems as waning, as being under control, or even as having disappeared. She experiences the transference as being resolved and can then form a mature and unencumbered relationship with her psychiatrist (9).

The following illustrates an example of a termination dream:

> A 35-year-old woman was in her third psychodynamic psychotherapy. Therapy had been started because of symptoms of anxiety and dysthymia. The patient reported a dream: "I am with you and we are having dinner. I comment that I am not feeling anxious and I am not sad. We have just finished discussing the problem I used to have—that I lacked confidence in myself. In the dream I remember that I felt quite capable, and when the check came, I insisted on paying it. Then we went outside, and I got in my car and drove away."

It will not surprise the reader that in associating to the elements of this dream, the patient brought up termination. Within a month a termination date had been set.

■ WORDS OF CAUTION

Some final words of caution: some patients are not particularly skilled at working with their dreams. No patient is able to work with dreams without being taught how and why, and no patient is able to work effectively with every dream. The examples in this chapter are obviously chosen for their clarity, but the psychotherapist must not be discouraged if only a small percentage of dream material proves useful to the process of uncovering what is outside the patient's conscious awareness. However, it is essential that this path to making conscious what is unconscious be tried in psychotherapy, because for some patients it will be a very useful method and for most patients it will be useful at least some of the time. By working with dreams, the patient can learn that dreams are another form of thinking that can be a part of the associations normally recalled in working on an area of conflict. For the therapist, there is no better way to learn how to work with dreams than to learn to understand one's own dreams in the context of understanding what is unconscious in oneself.

■ REFERENCES

1. Freud S: The interpretation of dreams (1900), in The Standard Edition of the Complete Psychological Works of Sigmund Freud, Vols 4 and 5. Translated and edited by Strachey J. London, Hogarth Press, 1953
2. Brenner C: Psychoanalytic Technique and Psychic Conflict. New York, International Universities Press, 1985
3. Grinberg L: Dreams and acting out. Psychoanal Q 56:155–176, 1987
4. Pulver SE: The manifest dream in psychoanalysis: a clarification. J Am Psychoanal Assoc 35:99–118, 1987
5. Palombo SR: Deconstructing the manifest dream. J Am Psychoanal Assoc 32:405–420, 1984
6. Gray P: Memory as resistance and the telling of a dream. J Am Psychoanal Assoc 40:307–326, 1992
7. Beratis S: The first analytic dream: mirror of the patient's neurotic conflicts and subsequent analytic process. Int J Psychoanal 65:461–469, 1984

8. Stimmel B: The written dream: action, resistance. and revelation. Psychoanal Q 64:658–671,1995

9. Cavenar JO Jr, Nash JL: The dream as a signal for termination. J Am Psychoanal Assoc 24:425–436, 1976

■ ADDITIONAL READINGS

Dowling S: Dreams and dreaming in relation to trauma in childhood. Int J Psychoanal 63:157–166, 1982

Palombo SR: Dreaming and Memory. New York, Basic Books, 1978

Sharpe EF: Dream Analysis. London, Hogarth Press, 1961

11

TERMINATION

Psychodynamic psychotherapy is often conducted in an open-ended fashion. The psychiatrist has explained to the patient that the treatment will take as long as required to discover and resolve the patient's unconscious core conflicts and for the patient to understand the workings of his mind. The treatment may continue for several years. As the relationship between the patient and the therapist deepens, more and more is understood. Change takes place by increments—often, hardly perceptible increments.

There comes a time, however, when the patient and the psychiatrist agree that it is time to end the treatment. At this juncture the troublesome areas of the patient's personality will seem to be separate from the core of the patient's sense of self (1). What was once central to the patient's presenting difficulties is now experienced as alien. The patient has learned to use intellect and perception in an affectively rich manner in the service of self-awareness (1).

■ RECOGNIZING WHEN THE TERMINATION PHASE IS APPROACHING

The therapist must remember and the patient must come to realize that treatment goals are related to, but different from, the patient's life goals (2). Treatment goals are always dependent to some extent on life's demands and possibilities—what is possible at a given time of life and in a given context. Termination does not mean a patient has realized all her hopes and wishes. Rather, the patient entering the end phase of treatment after a successful treatment will have experienced substantial relief of psychological suffering, and this relief will be evident to both the patient and the therapist. In addition, the internal conflicts of the patient, as well as the presenting symptoms, will have been resolved, and reasonably permanent changes in behavior will have occurred.

There are inevitably disappointments. Some persons will have lost educational, marital, or occupational opportunities because of age or life circumstances and will not, even after internal conflicts are resolved, be able to pursue what might have been desirable at a different time of life. These individuals, however, will have developed the psychological tools to understand and resolve conflict, will have understood how life has led them to this point, and will have mourned the lost hopes and desires.

As the end of the middle phase of treatment nears, the therapist will notice that the patient is able to understand her transferences in depth and recognize them in various settings (Table 11–1). The patient shows a detailed understanding of the working of her mind and is beginning to use self-inquiry as a method of problem solving. Often there will have been gains in most of these areas, although not necessarily all. The gains are observed by the therapist and shared with the patient as part of the patient's increasing awareness of new areas of strength and conflict resolution.

TABLE 11–1. **Criteria for termination of psychodynamic psychotherapy**

The patient

Experiences relief of symptoms.

Experiences symptoms as alien.

Understands his or her characteristic defenses.

Is able to understand and recognize his or her characteristic transference responses.

Engages in ongoing self-inquiry as a method of resolving internal conflicts.

During this time the patient and therapist are noting together that no new material is coming up and there do not appear to be any new resistances. Rather, the patient is working productively day in and day out using what has already been learned. Ideally, the patient raises termination as an issue. If it is very clear that termination is in the air and the patient avoids mentioning anything about the possibility, the therapist must approach this situation as a defense against the meaning of the termination. Frequently, once the patient has raised termination as a possibility, the therapist will want to listen for some time while the patient wades into this new stream. The therapist listens for the new issues and conflicts this topic raises and must determine whether this is a resistance or truly the point of sufficient therapeutic gain to warrant termination. Eventually the therapist will need to acknowledge to the patient his general concurrence: "Yes, it does seem we are getting close to that time." This will initiate a new series of thoughts and feelings for consideration in the treatment and will signal the beginning of the end of treatment. The termination date itself is set by mutual agreement. When the treatment has gone on for several years, that date may be several months off, sometimes as long as 6 months.

■ TASKS OF THE TERMINATION PHASE

There are four main tasks for the patient and the therapist during the termination phase (Table 11–2):

Review the Treatment

The patient reviews the treatment, reconsidering his history and conflicts and placing in perspective what has been learned. This aspect of termination involves a self-conscious effort to reflect with the therapist on what brought the patient into treatment and what has been learned about the patient's personality and developmental experience in the course of treatment. This process helps the patient complete the therapy with a sense of accomplishment.

TABLE 11–2.   **The work of termination**

The patient

Reviews the therapy.

Experiences and masters the separation and loss.

Reexperiences and remasters the transference.

Begins self-inquiry.

The patient and the therapist

Identify disappointments, limitations, and unsuccessful aspects of the therapy.

Discuss the possibility of future psychotherapy.

Discuss plans for the future.

This is usually a very affectively meaningful review of the work that the patient and therapist have done together. Frequently the patient experiences a feeling of pride, strength, and gratitude to the therapist in this process. This review also serves to aid the patient's future self-inquiry, refreshing the "table of contents" of the patient's knowledge about himself.

Experience the Loss of the Psychotherapy and the Therapist

In termination, the patient experiences what is an essential and poignant aspect of the human condition: the experience of separation—the loss of a relationship with a person who has been very helpful and who often is perceived as kind and understanding. The experience of loss becomes another opportunity for growth through identification of the feelings about transference figures awakened by this experience. The therapist also often feels an important loss at this time—a loss of a colleague and of a successful part of her work life. Careful attention to countertransference feelings is important at this time. The therapist may err by avoiding the experience of the patient's loss in whatever form it may appear or by accepting the feelings of loss as being completely real. In either case, transference elements may be inadvertently overlooked in the context of the therapist's and the patient's mutual self-regard.

Reexperience and Remaster the Transference

Very often, in the context of termination, there is a recrudescence of the patient's symptoms and a return of old transference patterns and styles of interacting with the therapist (3). The therapist should not be surprised or overly dismayed by this possibility. It can be an opportunity for the patient to exercise newfound skills and knowledge. In addition, the experience of separation evokes new and sometimes very important last transference elements related to the loss and to the recall of the hopes for magical reunion with the transference figures of childhood.

Increase Skills in Self-Inquiry as a Method of Problem Solving

The patient now begins to take over the functions of the therapist. In the best of circumstances, this becomes a lifelong process of self-inquiry. The patient increasingly exercises a greater degree of self-inquiry to resolve now well-known and -understood internal conflicts. This process requires that the therapist carefully direct and assist the patient, encouraging by not disturbing and by interpreting the transference resistances to these independent autonomous efforts.

Invariably, no matter how able and talented the patient, transference feelings have complicated the patient's ability to conduct his therapy. The patient has imbued the therapist with the authority of parental figures and looked to her for wisdom and perspective. Thus, the psychiatrist can be of inestimable aid by pointing out the residue of such transference feelings and the way they block the patient's enhanced ability to think independently about himself or herself, as the following example illustrates:

> A bright 35-year-old professional sought treatment because of difficulties in maintaining intimate relationships. After 3 years of treatment the patient was functioning much better at work and had become engaged to be married. A termination date was set for 6 months later. When the psychiatrist suggested that the patient review what he had learned in his treatment, the patient suddenly became very distant and expressed his belief that he might as well stop right away. He felt that a review was an intellectual challenge he could not meet. This transference response was quickly recognized by the patient and the analyst as another example of the kind of distancing behavior that had brought him into treatment and that he had always used to protect himself. However, this was the first time that this transference experience had led him to feel an inhibition in his intellectual ability. Recognizing this new form of the old transference, the patient then began to review the past therapy work and was able to carefully consider his feelings of sadness as his relationship to his psychiatrist drew to a close.

■ DISAPPOINTMENT IN THE TERMINATION PHASE

Disappointment is a part of life and a very important aspect of the experience of termination (4). The patient (and the therapist) must come to grips with what can never be. The therapist must recognize and acknowledge to himself the limitations of the treatment (Table 11–2). This recognition of the therapist's disappointment and its multiple sources is critical to the therapist's ability to work with the patient's disappointments in the therapy (5) and with the issue of termination in general.

At times the therapist does not want to end the treatment because of feeling disappointed with what has been accomplished or because of conscious or unconscious guilt about the patient's treatment. Both affection for the patient (6) and the sense of skillfulness the patient gives to the therapist by the successful therapy work can inhibit the therapist's ability to recognize and act at the time for termination. This can be experienced by the therapist as another form of disappointment around the issue of termination. The therapist's own reluctance to experience another separation and loss can also delay termination and can cause the therapist to overlook the patient's independent abilities. In all these instances, the therapist must carefully examine his sense of disappointment.

In some situations the termination may have been required by external events, either because the therapist is a trainee rotating off a service or because he works in a clinic where the length of treatment is limited or determined by medical insurance limitations. Of course the patient may also adamantly decide, despite good work on the therapist's part, to unilaterally and prematurely end the therapy. In all these situations the therapist may feel conscious difficulty in participating in the termination. The therapist's unconscious resistance to ending, which can be very multifaceted in some cases, may additionally complicate these terminations. Termination highlights the therapist's need to be alert to his own internal processes (7) in order to best help the patient.

In the termination phase, the therapist must be prepared to discuss tactfully and supportively the limitations of the treatment to prepare the patient to face the future realistically. The patient may ask, "Will I never feel so anxious again?" The patient usually raises, in some form, the issue of "What if I need more help?" The psychiatrist must help the patient to understand the transferential and the reality aspects of this question. The patient's plans for the future may realistically include the goal of further treatment when life circumstances change or new problems arise.

If it is clear that further treatment is indicated and this has been discussed, and if the patient does not explore this area, the therapist must address the patient's reluctance to appropriately take care of his or her health. The patient's wish to avoid further therapy or to prematurely reenter a new treatment requires attention in the termination phase. It is often helpful to patients who have been in a lengthy treatment to be told that the termination process actually extends beyond the last session. For some time after therapy stops, the patient will feel that she is still integrating aspects of the meaning of the termination. Frequently, these are parts of the feeling of being independent that can arise only when a patient is fully on her own. As already stated, the therapist's sense of loss and disappointment can serve as a block to the termination unless it is worked through. The following case illustrates this point:

A psychiatric trainee was completing his postgraduate training and was about to begin a private practice. He had been working for 2 years with an elementary school teacher who started therapy because of anxiety over working with young children. The therapy was not yet completed; however, the patient decided that he could not afford even the reduced fee the psychiatrist offered in order to continue their work in the private setting. The clinic in which the patient was seen had a policy of assigning trainees fresh intensive-therapy cases—that is, people who had not had prior experiences in therapy—so it was unlikely that this patient would soon have the chance to complete his psychotherapy. The doctor and the patient worked hard during the termination phase. The patient looked back effectively on what had been done together.

Yet it was clear to the doctor that much more needed to be accomplished. The doctor developed a sense of profound sadness, guilt, and even a related obsessive-compulsive handwashing symptom. He went to the clinic director, an experienced psychoanalyst, who arranged for him to enter psychotherapy with a very skilled and senior psychoanalyst. Fairly quickly the psychiatrist came to understand the roots of his guilt in his own childhood experience and the ways in which his feelings made it harder for his patient to come to grips with his own feelings about further therapy. In effect, the patient felt sad and stuck, as did the therapist. Indeed, once the therapist recognized all this, his work with his patient improved, the patient was able to decide to get a weekend job, and although he still could not afford his therapist's reduced fees, the patient planned to save his money and restart treatment in the future.

■ WHEN THE TREATMENT IS UNSUCCESSFUL

So far the cases and situations that have been described have had relatively happy endings. But there are some cases where the treatment simply does not work. The therapist may decide that the treatment will not work and that termination is necessary, or the patient may decide to terminate despite an interpretation of resistance and advice to the contrary. In such cases the patient, the therapist, or both may not only be disappointed but quite angry—sometimes at each other, sometimes at themselves, and sometimes at those whose theories, promises, or teachings had led them to expect a more successful outcome.

There are no simple answers as to how such situations are to be handled. Certainly, it is important that the therapist work to create an atmosphere in which disappointment and anger can be expressed by the patient. If at all possible, the patient should be helped to consider alternative treatments or treatment settings. To be sure, a common problem for both inexperienced and experienced psychodynamic psychotherapists is that, because they place a high value on this form of treatment, they invariably convey to their patients the idea that if the treatment does not work there has been a failure. Indeed, there may be no way to avoid a sense of failure in working with certain patients, because no matter how neutral the therapist has been, without conveying some measure of therapeutic enthusiasm and optimism, psychodynamic psychotherapy would almost certainly never get off the ground.

Yet there are certain attitudes that the psychiatrist can convey in the termination phase of a very unsuccessful therapy that may help to reduce the patient's sense of failure. First, the psychiatrist must remember that the patient is an ever-changing individual, regardless of specific personality traits and psychological problems. Patients who have not had successful therapy at one point in their lives may at some time in the future have successful therapy. If the therapist understands this and states it to the patient, it can not only lessen the patient's sense of failure but also enhance the chance that the patient will seek future treatment. Similarly, there is much that is unknown about therapeutic fit—the match between psychiatrist and patient. Again, if the psychiatrist understands this variable and conveys it thoughtfully to the patient, a kind of no-fault attitude can result, and the patient may again seek treatment with a different therapist. Finally, the frank discussion of such matters in termination might, in some cases, lead to an unexpected request for referral to another psychotherapist, or to the mutual realization that transfer, and not termination, is in order. Inevitably there are treatment failures, as with any medical treatment. In such cases the supportive, long-term, nondogmatic, and caring attitude of the psychiatrist will go a long way toward minimizing the negative effects of the experience and maximizing the possibility of future efforts at treatment.

■ WHEN THE PATIENT REFUSES TO TERMINATE DESPITE SUCCESSFUL TREATMENT

Sometimes psychodynamic psychotherapists are puzzled because a treatment seems to have gone well but a patient never brings up termination, even indirectly. The therapist listens for hints and pays particular attention to the symbolic meaning of dreams and day-dreams but finds nothing that helps to understand why termination is not mentioned.

In these situations a patient is usually wishing not to terminate for one or more very specific reasons: a fantasy that is gratified by the ongoing therapy, which originates in childhood; a fear of losing the person of the therapist as she exists within that fantasy; a fear of an affect directed at the departing therapist as she exists in that fantasy; and a hope for the realization of a long-held wish for the therapist as she exists within that fantasy. A concrete example will illustrate this point.

> A businessman in his thirties came for therapy because of anxiety and unhappiness. Much of the therapeutic inquiry focused on depriving early parental relationships, which, he came to see, had left him with poor internal controls of affect, chronic anticipation of disappointment, and frequent feelings of sadness about his own achievements. After 3 years of twice-weekly psychodynamic psychotherapy he was able to better understand and regulate his affects and no longer felt particularly anxious or unhappy. But he never spoke of ending the therapy. His psychiatrist began to wonder about this but came up with no ideas about what was going on.
>
> The patient had for some time been enjoying a much improved social life. Now he became interested in a co-worker but reported that she was married. At first the psychiatrist thought little of this, but slowly, as his patient's interest in this woman turned into an obsession, he began to wonder where it might fit into the transference, how it might explain the transference. Eventually, the therapist began to hear in the patient's associations many

hints that this unavailable woman represented the therapist (a cross-gender transference) as well as the patient's mother. The therapist began to develop a hypothesis: that termination never came up because the psychiatrist was experienced by the patient as a gratifying mother, that the patient feared his own rage at his mother (the therapist) should they separate (terminate), and that there existed a fantasy in the patient that the therapy, representing a special union with the mother of the patient's childhood, would last forever. Careful listening confirmed and refined this set of ideas, and appropriate interpretations were formulated and offered. The patient came to understand his fantasy, and eventually he lost interest in his married woman friend and began a termination phase in his therapy. This process, up to the start of the termination phase, lasted for most of a year.

■ LEAVETAKING: THE REACTIONS OF THE THERAPIST

The termination phase of psychodynamic psychotherapy involves a leavetaking that for both the patient and the psychiatrist is emotionally demanding. The richness of the psychodynamic relationship is remarkable, for it is fundamentally an experience of psychological growth and development, touching deeply both the patient and the psychiatrist. That both members of the dyad have been involved in this experience of growth is inevitable. For the patient, therapy is structured to create this possibility; for the psychotherapist, the depth of the relationship and the experience of helping another person to a second chance at maturation invariably lead to new self-understanding and change. So, in the end, whereas the terminating patient has been helped to recognize all the issues of termination and to discuss them with the therapist, the therapist may be left with a range of complex and contradictory feelings.

Termination is one of the most demanding aspects of the treatment for the therapist. The therapist's experience of termination has recently been the focus of attention of psychodynamic clinicians and writers (5). It is essential that the psychiatrist who offers this form of treatment expect to experience strong reactions and that he specifically and carefully explore the related feelings and thoughts. Lingering feelings of loss, pleasure at personal growth, and fantasies about future meetings with the patient are all commonplace in the therapist at termination and must be privately understood. It is essential that these feelings be consciously recognized and understood, for when the last good-bye is spoken, patients never stop needing to know, and must be explicitly informed, that the former therapist is a potential future therapy resource. If the therapist does not explore his reactions to the termination, such an assurance may not be given or may lack authority. That is not to say that former therapists cannot greet former patients in natural ways, should they meet by chance. But the psychiatrist should preserve for the patient the possibility of returning for future assistance by ending the treatment with the appropriate therapeutic boundaries intact. It is also important for the psychiatrist to preserve intact the patient's memory of a satisfactory experience of closure in therapy, for this memory can be used as a model when the patient solves new problems in the future (8). In this regard, for example, going to former patients for contributions for favorite charities or professional advice can greatly affect the patient's view of the therapeutic work and the patient's experience of the therapist's future availability. The grateful former patient may not be able to refuse a request; but, filled with resentment, he may not be able to return to the therapist for help or to use memories of a successful treatment as a model for future problem solving.

The psychodynamic psychotherapist can be helped with the intensity of the feelings of termination through self-inquiry. Both understanding the meaning of the relationship to his patient and being familiar with the limitations of treatment can aid the processing of the therapist's responses (Table 11–3). Supervision and

Table 11–3.	**Techniques to help the psychotherapist during the termination of treatment**

The disciplined practice of self-inquiry

Familiarity with the limitations of psychodynamic psychotherapy

Supervision and consultation

Personal psychoanalysis or in-depth psychodynamic psychotherapy

discussion with colleagues can often provide insight and remove the sense of isolation. Personal psychoanalysis or in-depth psychodynamic psychotherapy is an invaluable aid to understanding one's own responses to this emotionally intense phase of the treatment.

■ REFERENCES

1. Alexander F: The voice of the intellect is soft. Psychoanal Rev 28:12–29, 1941
2. Ticho E: Termination of psychoanalysis: treatment goals, life goals. Psychoanal Q 41:315–333, 1972
3. Gillman RD: The termination phase in psychoanalytic practice: a survey of 48 completed cases. Psychoanalytic Inquiry 2:463–472, 1982
4. Novick J: Termination: themes and issues. Psychoanalytic Inquiry 2:329–365, 1982
5. Viorst J: Experiences of loss at the end of analysis: the analyst's response to termination. Psychoanalytic Inquiry 2:399–418, 1982
6. Coen SJ: Barriers to love between patient and analyst. J Am Psychoanal Assoc 42:1107–1135, 1994
7. Buxbaum E: Technique of terminating analysis. Int J Psychoanal 31:184–190, 1950
8. Pfeffer AZ: After the analysis: analyst as both old and new object. J Am Psychoanal Assoc 41: 323–337, 1993

■ ADDITIONAL READINGS

Dewald PA: The clinical importance of the termination phase. Psychoanalytic Inquiry 2:441–461, 1982

Firestein SK: Termination in Psychoanalysis. New York, International Universities Press, 1978

Reich A: On the termination of psychoanalysis. Int J Psychoanal 31:179–183, 1950

12

PRACTICAL PROBLEMS AND THEIR MANAGEMENT

All therapists face practical problems in the use of psychodynamic psychotherapy. For the beginning therapist these issues can frequently feel like a Rubik's cube—a multifaceted puzzle, for which there appears to be no solution (Table 12–1). These issues range from the very basic—such as choosing the office and its decor, arranging fees, dealing with medical insurance, handling telephone calls, and scheduling vacations—to the more difficult topics of suicidal and dangerous patients, whether to accept gifts, when to give patients advice, how to handle illness in the patient, boundaries, managed-care intrusions, and how to handle one's own mistakes.

■ THE OFFICE: DECOR AND SETTING

The office decor should be simple and comfortable, neither too sterile and impersonal nor too intrusively informative about the therapist's private life. Pictures of a therapist's family members should be avoided. Patients' transferences frequently include thoughts about the therapist's family—parents, spouse, and children. Concrete information about those people can be a block to both the timing and the content of a patient's fantasies about these parts of the therapist's life. If a patient is seriously disturbed, the patient's knowing intimate details of the therapist's life can also make the therapist needlessly anxious. If a patient has knowledge of the therapist's life, countertransference reactions can also become more intense, because the patient's fantasies may be built

TABLE 12–1.	**Common practical problems in psychodynamic psychotherapy**
Office decor and setting	Pharmacotherapy
Dangerous patients	Telephone calls
Fees	Illness in the patient
Gifts	Scheduling vacations
Medical insurance/managed care	Therapist errors
Advice giving	Suicidal patients

closer to the realities of the therapist's life as revealed in family pictures and mementos in the office. The patient may also feel knowing about the therapist's outside life as a burden, making it difficult for the patient to express intense feelings.

Office lighting should be adequate but not harsh. A very dimly lit room may be felt as seductive by the patient; a too brightly lit room may feel uncomfortably sterile. Therapists should avoid sitting behind the barrier of a desk. Comfortable chairs should be available for both the patient and the therapist. The chairs should be arranged at a distance that provides intimacy without intrusiveness.

Patients are seen in a variety of settings, including hospital or clinic offices, offices in office buildings, and home offices. Obviously, potentially acting-out psychotic or dangerous patients are optimally treated in a hospital or clinic setting where help can be close at hand.

There are special guidelines for the use of a home office, because, by definition, patients are given access to a considerable amount of personal information about the therapist who sees patients in the home office. Potential patients for a home office should be screened very carefully over the telephone. Patients with histories of violence, psychotic transferences, or character disorders involving acting out should not be seen in a home office. The intense transferences developed by these patients, combined with their poor ego controls and tendency to take action, can frequently result in an intrusion into the life of the therapist and the therapist's family that makes treatment uncomfortable for the therapist and sometimes untenable. Such patients may repeatedly drive past the therapist's home, follow a therapist's family members, or generally experience an overwhelming temptation to abuse the therapist's privacy.

Over the telephone a therapist may ask a prospective patient the following questions:

1. What are the symptoms you need help with now?
2. Have you been in psychotherapy before?
3. Have you been on medications for a psychiatric problem, and if so, which ones? (The answers to this question may provide a clue to diagnosis, especially if antipsychotic agents have been prescribed.)
4. Have you ever been hospitalized? In what circumstances?

The organization, discretion, appropriateness, and coherence with which a patient contacts a prospective therapist over the telephone are all good clues to the appropriateness of using a home office setting for a particular patient. For example, a person who calls a therapist from across town and feels it is urgent to see that particular therapist because of an article in the newspaper about the therapist's work may not be the best home office patient. This person may well be indicating his or her tendency to form a rapid, intense, and irrational transference. A patient who obtains the therapist's name in the process of requesting a referral from a physician or other appropriate source, such as a friend or relative, will make a better home office patient.

The convenience to the therapist of the home office is counter-balanced by the risks of an intensified transference and a consequent defensive and overly self-protective countertransference.

The therapist needs to feel that the boundaries around home, family, and private life are secure.

■ FEES

Outside hospitals and clinics with free care and sliding-scale fees, the psychotherapist in private practice generally charges a fee dictated by the standards of his locality. Fees need to be treated in a matter-of-fact, consistent way from the very beginning of treatment. Many patients, perhaps the majority, have conflicts about money. These conflicts will enter into the material of the psychotherapy. Money very frequently becomes associated with issues of dependency, emotional supplies, and feelings of guilt, avarice, deprivation, or entitlement. The psychotherapist should be direct and clear about issues of the fee.

Therapists differ in their views of fees and how they think about their billing. Medical insurance and managed-care relationships have further complicated an already complicated issue. Ongoing long-term psychotherapy patients are at times seen, in effect, as "renting" hours in the schedules of their therapists and therefore, in general, paying for missed appointments unless they are otherwise filled or rescheduled. In many ways this policy is the most neutral and fundamentally respectful stance for the therapist to take. Otherwise, the therapist takes the position of making a moral judgment about whether the absence was justified. In such a case, the therapist, in effect, volunteers to make a personal financial sacrifice if an absence is deemed worthy of being excused. If the patient is angered by paying for a missed hour, there is then an opportunity to explore the dynamics of the anger and why the patient feels that the therapist should absorb the exigencies of the patient's life. Similarly, the therapist operating on these guidelines can more appropriately set fees reflecting a known stability of chargeable hours and therefore a potentially lower per-session fee.

None of this is to say that a therapist should not set lower fees for a given patient if it makes sense and feels comfortable to do so.

Every therapist should determine beforehand his personal financial limits. Clinicians should be candid with themselves about how difficult a given patient will be. Clinicians should also determine how much they need to feel their own professional work time is being valued, as well as whether they feel a physician should donate part of his time. In general, therapists review their fees with patients yearly, at which time they may adjust for cost-of-living increases. Therapists may also adjust upward the fees of patients who have been paying lower fees as the patients' financial circumstances permit. Low-fee patients frequently feel both infantilized and special. Also, the patient paying a low fee may feel obligated to take care of the therapist in other ways, such as not getting angry at the therapist. These feelings must be dealt with interpretively by the therapist.

The therapist's usual way of handling fees, especially policies about insurance, billing, and planned reviews and increases, should be clearly discussed with patients at the end of the evaluation and before beginning psychotherapy. If it is the therapist's policy to treat sessions as rented time, the patient will need an explanation of why he is charged for sessions if he does not attend. The description of renting hours is frequently helpful. It is sometimes also helpful to encourage patients to think in terms of monthly or yearly cost rather than cost per hour. If it is comfortable for the therapist, the possibility of paying the bill for treatment after termination over an extended time can also be discussed. For a brief psychotherapy this may be a very practical solution and in keeping with the patient's expectations of other medical procedures.

The patient always has the right to seek a different therapist because of financial reasons or a difference of opinion on the manner of scheduling and charging for appointments. In such a case the therapist should assist the patient in finding another therapist or treatment setting that will more closely match the patient's desires. Objections that appear to be based on conflict or neurosis can be addressed through exploration and interpretation in an extended evaluation. However, because it is early in the treatment and the patient has not yet formed a solid therapeutic alliance with the therapist, this method is frequently not successful.

■ MEDICAL INSURANCE AND MANAGED CARE

In the present-day climate of third-party payers and managed care, the therapist often is in the position of dealing with insurance agencies and case managers. These situations are often complicated. To the extent practicable, the therapist should be available to complete forms, reports, etc., but she should let the patient deal with and bill the insurance company. This is not always possible with patients who have few resources. When required to write a review of a case and submit it to the insurance company, the patient's permission should always be requested in writing and the patient's desire should be followed. Many therapists will go over any report with the patient before sending 't in or will at least ask the patient if he wants to do so. There should be nothing new to the patient in such a report. Because in general these reports document symptoms and problem areas rather than psychodynamic hypotheses and unconscious formulations, in practice reviewing the report with the patient is less troublesome than it might seem and sometimes stimulates important dialogue.

When a case manager has refused continued treatment, the therapist should discuss the situation with the patient and describe the options available. It is important that the therapist inform the patient of the recommended course of treatment and the alternatives with their pros and cons, regardless of a case manager's decision. The therapist should always be prepared to appeal a case manager's decision and work with the patient to explain the case in detail and the indications for treatment. When there is a protracted disagreement with the case manager's perspective and appeal is not effective, the impact on treatment can be substantial. The patient may worry, appropriately, about his illness and his need for treatment. The therapist must aid the patient in seeing realistic limitations and possible contractual abuses by insurers or managed-care providers without encouraging the patient's acting out or becoming the vehicle of the therapist's own fears, anger, and disappointments. The focus of the therapy may well become understanding the patient's conflicts as they are evidenced in dealing with the process of appropriately protecting oneself and seeking resolution of insurer or managed-care disagreements.

■ PHARMACOTHERAPY

Combined treatments using both psychotherapy and medication are the norm rather than the exception. These two treatment strategies tend to be complementary. Medication primarily affects specific symptoms but is generally less effective on interpersonal patterns, social skills, and defense patterns that affect rehabilitation, compliance, and long term successful outcome. Both transference and countertransference issues must be closely observed in the medication process. The patient may see medication as meaning she can "just wait for it to work" and as an indication of the physician's power. Alternatively, the patient may have particular fantasies about the type of medication use: "My mom was on that medicine." Such a statement has both biological importance (e.g.,indicating a medication likely to be useful) and psychodynamic meaning (e.g.,to take the medicine means to become like mother). The exploration of these areas can be important to understanding the patient's conflicts and to ensuring medication compliance.

The physician prescribing medication may also be more likely to experience countertransference feelings related to the patient's resistance. The physician may experience the patient as refusing medication rather than as expressing a resistance that would yield either to interpretation or to further information about the medication. The patient needs clear information about the indications and side effects of medication. The psychotherapeutic relationship encourages a cooperative decision-making process in the choice of medications and how long to continue them.

■ TELEPHONE CALLS

When patients telephone their therapists between appointments, the general rule is to accept the call or to return calls promptly and to listen carefully, with an eye to keeping these between-session conversations brief. Interpretations over the telephone should be avoided. The reason for the call should be explored and interpreted in the very next session. The therapist should be clear that communication and exploration are meant to be confined to the scheduled appointment. If, however, there is an emergency, the therapist needs to respond by any means necessary. Such emergencies may arise with the following:

- A psychotic or suicidal patient
- Voluntary or involuntary commitment
- A patient dangerous to self or others for whom the police need to be alerted and dispatched
- An acute medical emergency in which the psychotherapist needs to make the appropriate, immediate medical referral

It is most important that in an emergency the matter be dealt with directly and rapidly. Any possible interpretations of the patient's call should be postponed to a calmer moment in a subsequent session.

In emergencies, it may also be possible to hold a planned session over the telephone. This is most effective in a well-developed therapy where the subtleties of communication are well known by the patient and the therapist. For a patient unexpectedly confined to home with an illness, during intense times in the treatment when vacations or travel make meeting in the office impossible, or in rural areas or overseas when no local resources are available, a telephone session may be very helpful. The lack of personal contact is, however, a severe constraint on the patient's experience of the treatment and the information available to the therapist; therefore telephone sessions should be used cautiously. Telemedicine may offer unique opportunities for psychotherapy in the future as both voice and real-time video are combined at reasonable cost. Telemedicine has already been used in disaster situations to good effect.

■ SCHEDULING VACATIONS

Patients should be told as far in advance as possible of a therapist's vacation dates. On-call coverage should always be arranged with a colleague for patients who are judged to need to have someone available. Sick or acutely disturbed patients may require actual appointments with the on-call therapist; these visits should be arranged before the therapist leaves town. In some circumstances a patient may need to reach a vacationing therapist, but in general this should be unnecessary and should be discouraged.

Patients' reactions to vacations provide an opportunity to explore reactions to separation as well as reactions to opportunities for independence and play. A therapist's absence can trigger memories of important earlier separations and can provide an opportunity for a patient to consolidate previous therapeutic gains and experience greater autonomy.

■ SUICIDAL PATIENTS

The assessment of suicidal potential and the prevention of suicide attempts are major concerns to the therapist in training and remain important issues in the professional life of the psychotherapist. A careful history is the best guide when judging suicidal risk. Patients who have attempted suicide in the past are definitely at risk, at least for feeling suicidal again over the course of an intensive psychotherapy (assuming that the critical associated conflicts are explored in treatment). Also, patients who have actually attempted to harm themselves, even in the distant past, are as a rule at greater risk than patients who have felt suicidal without taking action. A history of suicidal feelings should always be respected and treated as a serious and important concern, never dismissed as "merely" manipulative.

In order to handle periods of suicidal feelings in the course of a patient's treatment, the therapist should be alert and prepared. In general, when a therapist is worried that a patient may be feeling suicidal, it is wiser to inquire frankly than to withhold the question out of a fear of being tactless or too disturbing. A potentially suicidal patient is generally reassured to know that the therapist is aware, concerned, and not shocked by the patient's feelings. Other helpful strategies include these:

- Having a firm contract with a patient that he will call for help if in danger of taking suicidal action
- Having on-call therapist coverage for nights, weekends, and vacations
- Knowing where one can hospitalize a patient quickly in an emergency

Letting a patient know that the therapist is prepared to hospitalize the patient can often, paradoxically, go a long way toward allaying the need to hospitalize in some cases. If a psychotherapist has a high level of concern about a suicidal patient, it is important to know where family members can be reached. If a patient seriously considers and verbalizes a specific suicidal plan of action, the therapist is obligated to consider whether the moment for notifying the family and instituting involuntary commitment proceedings has come.

■ DANGEROUS PATIENTS

Patients who have harmed others and/or who express rage and impulses to harm their therapists and others are a challenge to any psychotherapist. The guiding rule for psychotherapists is not to attempt to be a hero. Therapists are obliged to notify both potential victims of violence and the authorities if a serious risk is present. Therapists also need to feel that they themselves are working in an environment that protects their own safety. With a tense or threatening patient, the therapist should never block the door or make it difficult for the enraged patient to exit quickly. Such patients may best be seen in a hospital, clinic, or group practice setting where help is quickly available and both the patient and the therapist can feel safe enough to explore the difficult issues creating the patient's rage.

■ GIFTS

Whether to accept a gift from a patient is a sticky problem that comes up in virtually every practice. The ideal would be to not accept a gift but to explore the wishes and fantasies behind the patient's desire to give the gift. However, sometimes with fragile patients the blow to self-esteem resulting from refusing a gift outweighs any advantage gained by refusing it. Judicious clinical judgment is required in these cases. A gift may be accepted, especially if understanding and interpreting the meaning of the gift becomes a part of the treatment. Obviously, if the patient wishes to make a gift of an expensive item, such presents cannot ethically be accepted. Gifts are an example of the general problem of maintaining boundaries in psychotherapy. Overall, one wants to choose the course of action that keeps the patient able to express the widest array of feelings and does not inhibit the patient's associations—as a result either of the patient's feeling special or of his losing the feeling that he matters to the therapist.

■ ADVICE GIVING: THE PSYCHOTHERAPIST AS PHYSICIAN

The psychodynamic psychotherapist tries, in general, to adhere to a neutral, empathic, nondirective stance with the patient. Rare situations and emergencies arise in which the therapist should appropriately give advice to a patient. An unrecognized medical emergency would be one example in which a therapist is correct to give medical advice. For example, if the therapy patient reports a black, tarry stool (suggesting intestinal hemorrhage) or visual and neurological anomalies (suggesting an intracranial emergency), the patient may be totally unaware of the importance of these symptoms, and the therapist should provide direct, clear advice on how to proceed to have the symptoms evaluated. Occasionally a patient with psychophysiological disease may require emergency referral and coordination with medical specialists. For example, one patient with granulomatous colitis hemorrhaged during a period of enraged transference with her psychotherapist. Many such patients have symptoms that express their more conflicted and difficult affects somatically for many months and even years until they begin to acknowledge and express their feelings consciously and verbally. For the patient just discussed, working closely with her internist provided the best environment for her overall health and safety.

An emergency in a patient's family, including dangerous activities of children, may also require advice. At other times it is appropriate to provide a medical or psychiatric referral for someone in the patient's life. Occasionally it also becomes important to point out to patients that they are putting themselves in great financial or medical jeopardy by continuing to pursue a particular course of action either out of naivete or out of unconscious self-destructiveness.

All of these events require tact and thoughtfulness. In the well-conducted psychotherapy that reaches sufficient depth, the meaning of these events, including the physician's interventions, will be explored and understood. It is important to remember that the physician-therapist's decision to advise or the decision not to advise must be eventually explored with the patient and its meaning and points of contact with the past examined.

■ ILLNESS IN THE PATIENT

Any significant illness in the patient that requires hospitalization or missing a large number of sessions should be directly addressed. The patient and/or the therapist may prefer to stop the treatment and free the therapist's hour, planning to restart the treatment later. The best guide in such cases is the therapist's role as physician who keeps in mind the best interests of the patient. Sending a card to a patient in the hospital if a serious illness arises can be an important aspect of maintaining the therapeutic alliance and of physicianly concern.

■ THERAPIST ERRORS

When the therapist makes a mistake—such as forgetting a session, double-scheduling an hour, or making an error on a bill—the therapist should acknowledge the error, apologize if appropriate, and then seek out the patient's feelings about the event. Frequently patients do not want to acknowledge that the therapist made a mistake, or they do not want to acknowledge the anger and hurt they feel at being slighted. The therapist must also use such events as an opportunity for self-inquiry to understand the meaning of such a slip. Understanding these countertransference attitudes can at times help the therapist see subtle aspects of the patient that the therapist had been overlooking but was responding to unconsciously because of similarities to an event in his own past.

■ GENERAL GUIDELINES

The possible practical problems are innumerable. However, some guidelines emerge for the general management of such events (Table 12–2). First, in a medical emergency, either for the patient or for a member of the patient's family (e.g., a violent patient or imminent child abuse), do what must be done. Similarly, in medical

---

TABLE 12–2. **General guidelines for the management of practical problems in psychodynamic psychotherapy**

In a medical emergency, "do what must be done."

Both action and inaction require exploration.

Operate as a concerned physician.

Foster autonomy and independence.

Create a setting of safety to allow for exploration.

---

illness, the patient can be referred for treatment, and then the dynamic issues of how the patient seeks care or avoids it can be dealt with as well as how she felt about asking for the referral. In general, after a practical issue has been managed, it must be remembered by the therapist and its echoes observed and explored in the therapy. Both action and inaction require exploring the meaning to the patient. There is no one right answer. Frequently, operating as the concerned physician who wants to foster the autonomy of the patient and not put her at undue risk will head the psychiatrist in the direction that will maintain the alliance with the patient and allow for an event to be explored later on. The psychotherapist should keep in mind the overall goal of treatment: to allow the patient to explore her feelings, fantasies, and behaviors in an ever-deepening manner. This goal can provide guidance in handling most practical problems both during and subsequent to the acute events. Finally, the psychodynamic psychotherapist orients to doing what will best allow for the verbal exploration of feelings, thoughts, and behaviors in a safe setting.

■ SUGGESTED READINGS

Beitman BD, Klerman GL (eds): Integrating Pharmacotherapy and Psychotherapy. Washington, DC, American Psychiatric Press, 1991

Epstein RS: Keeping Boundaries: Maintaining Safety and Integrity in the Psychotherapeutic Process. Washington, DC, American Psychiatric Press, 1994

Gabbard GO: Psychodynamic Psychiatry in Clinical Practice: The DSM IV Edition. Washington, DC, American Psychiatric Press, 1994

Schwartz HJ (ed); Psychodynamic Concepts in General Psychiatry. Washington, DC, American Psychiatric Press, 1995

13

BRIEF PSYCHOTHERAPY

Following World War II there was rapid growth in the demand for psychotherapy. With the community mental health movement and the more recent cost consciousness of health care, the interest in brief psychodynamic psychotherapy has greatly increased. Brief psychotherapy is now a necessary part of every clinician's skills. This treatment modality requires the therapist to confront her own ambitiousness and perfectionism and any idealized picture of personality function. Brief psychodynamic psychotherapy is directed to behavioral change in a focused area of conflict. It is distinguished from longer-term psychodynamic psychotherapy by the time limits placed on the treatment. The limited time gives the treatment its unique characteristics—goals, selection of patients, and treatment techniques.

Brief psychotherapy aims the treatment at the continuity of the patient's development that has been stymied by the emergence of a psychodynamic conflict affecting the life course. Through focusing on this central conflict, which is the point of most urgency in the patient's current life, and on the way in which this conflict is critical in the patient's life, the therapist hopes to make changes that will affect the full range of the growth and development of the patient. Often this focus can be identified as a pattern of relating that includes expectations, fantasies, and assumptions formed from the pattern of relating to a significant person in childhood. (In a number of empirical studies, this pattern has recently been called the core conflictual relationship theme [1].)

Whereas longer-term psychotherapy focuses on the shared past, brief psychodynamic psychotherapy relies upon the propitious moment (2), a moment in the patient's life when he is particularly open to change because of the intensity and acuteness of the present conflict. Because of its brevity, brief psychodynamic psychotherapy relies more heavily than longer-term psychotherapy on the patient's own ability to practice, generalize, and apply what is gained in the therapeutic work to multiple examples that occur after treatment. This critical difference between brief and long-term psychodynamic psychotherapy means that the patient must have the ability to practice and work through much of the conflict on his own once the pattern of the problems (defenses and transference distortions) is identified.

Freud's original analyses were quite short, lasting 3 to 6 months. Over time, however, analysis has become a much longer procedure. Franz Alexander (3) was one of the early workers in brief psychodynamic psychotherapy. More recently, the work of David Malan (4), Peter Sifneos (5), James Mann (6), and Habib Davanloo (7) has formed the basis of present-day treatment. Although there are differences in these authors' selection criteria and techniques, their areas of agreement are much more striking (8, 9).

■ SELECTION OF PATIENTS

Identifying the focal conflict is the sine qua non of brief psychodynamic psychotherapy. In addition, the patient must have a capacity to think in feeling terms and be highly motivated. The more specific the chief complaint, the more likely it is that the conflict area will be able to be dealt with in a brief time (10). Complex or deep-seated issues require more time. The patient who reports at least one meaningful relationship with another person during her life will have better object relationships and be better able to tolerate the difficult feelings that can be stirred by the psychotherapy (Table 13–1). A good response to a trial interpretation is also a good prognostic sign. Malan emphasizes that if the therapist cannot make affective contact with the patient, it will be difficult to form

TABLE 13–1. **Patient selection for brief psychodynamic psychotherapy**

Patient:

Focal conflict

Able to think in feeling terms

Highly motivated

At least one meaningful relationship

Good response to trial interpretation

Therapist:

Able to make affective contact with the patient

Excludes patients with severe depression, psychosis, or acting out

Usually excludes patients who have borderline or narcissistic personality disorders or paranoid disorders

a therapeutic alliance in the short time available for brief psychotherapy.

Sifneos stresses the importance of a focus that is oedipal in nature—usually meaning involving a competitive theme around success, winning, losing, and becoming "bigger." However, other authors allow for a broader range of developmental origins of the focal conflict. Although severity of illness per se is not a criterion, many of the selection criteria exclude patients with serious pathology. If one anticipates the possibility of severe depressive or psychotic episodes or if the patient tends to act out his or her pathology (e.g., substance abuse, suicidal behavior), the patient is not suitable for a time-limited treatment, which cannot provide the flexible support that may be needed. Similarly, projection, splitting, and denial make it difficult to form a therapeutic alliance in a short time, a requirement of brief psychotherapy work. This limitation means that borderline, narcissistic, and paranoid patients will not usually do well in brief psychodynamic psychotherapy.

The selection of the focus is the most important part of the evaluation for brief psychodynamic psychotherapy. The majority of therapists will not undertake a brief psychodynamic psychotherapy unless a focus becomes clear during the evaluation. The precipitant, early life traumas, and repetitive patterns of behavior can point the way to the central focus. Occasionally a dream may be reported that the patient recognizes as important and may hold the opening to the focal conflict. It is the congruence between the current life conflict and the childhood conflict that is sought. The greater the chance that the conflict can emerge and be analyzed in the transference, the more likely it is that the treatment can reach a successful conclusion. Frequently, more than one possible focal conflict area is identifiable. It is the skill of the therapist that is used in deciding which focal area is most critical to deal with and will be most accessible—that is, able to be dissected out from the other aspects of the personality (9).

The focal conflict should be presented to the patient at the end of the evaluation phase as part of proposing the beginning of a brief psychodynamic psychotherapy. It should be phrased in the everyday language of the patient. Mann describes the core conflict as the present and chronically endured pain of the patient that is preconscious. This is usually identified by the patient's feeling glad, sad, mad, frightened or guilty (7). The central issue specifies the therapeutic contract and the goal of the treatment, as in the following example:

> A 41-year-old married man, a successful midlevel manager, sought evaluation because of increasing marital problems. He described his interest in his marriage as having decreased greatly over the past several years. Marital discord had become a prominent part of the relationship with his wife. He had a son, aged 12, whom he wanted to make "stand up for himself." When his son and wife argued, he withdrew. Sexually he felt much less interest in his wife than he had, and he found himself

more interested in *Playboy* types of magazines. In taking the past history, the therapist learned that the patient's father had committed suicide when the patient was 12 years old. The father had been employed in a line of work similar to the patient's. The patient's mother was quiet and reserved. She had not remarried until 10 years before the patient entered therapy, and her second husband died 5 years after the marriage in a plane crash.

What are the potential focal conflicts in this patient? One might be the moving away from intimacy (with his wife) and turning to a more self-contained style. The fact that his son is near the age the patient was when his father killed himself is prominent, and it may lead the way to exploring the feelings of loss at the death of his father. However, the patient is also about to outlive his father. Another focal area, different from loss, would be his conflicted feelings of triumph at outliving his father. In this case the transference might be paternal and competitive. When he sees his wife and son arguing, the patient may also be reexperiencing his own difficulties in having been raised by his mother. Working with this focal conflict might reveal a maternal transference.

Thus in this case there are potentially multiple active conflict areas. Which to select is the clinician's task. Although selection is never an easy task, some guidelines can be helpful (Table 13–2). The chosen conflict area should be active. A trial interpretation of an active conflict will frequently elicit great emotion, an index of an active conflict area. Beginning therapists often overlook the fears of success a patient brings, finding it easier to empathize with loss than with fears of success. It is helpful always to formulate a case from a fear-of-success perspective as well as from a loss perspective so that conflicts over success are not overlooked. Brief psychotherapy, because of its short duration and its always impending separation, tends to highlight past conflicts related to loss. If these are oedipal losses, rather than enmeshed preoedipal rela-

TABLE 13–2.	Identifying the focal conflict in psychodynamic psychotherapy

Identify the conflicts:

Explore the precipitant, early life traumas, and repetitive behaviors for conflict patterns.

Look for areas of inhibition.

Be alert to conflicts about success as well as about loss.

Choose one focal conflict:

Choose a conflict that is active in the patient's life.

Make a trial interpretation of the conflict, which often elicits an affective response.

Choose a conflict related to one transference figure.

tionships, the therapy frequently lends itself well to their exploration. In any single brief psychotherapy, only one conflict area should be dealt with. In general, this means the transference will center around one person, and the focal conflict should be formulated to the patient about that one person. Transference interpretations should be limited to that one significant person of the past. Avoid going all over the map. Conflicts that cause inhibitions should be particularly looked for. Addressing conflict areas that have caused inhibition will allow the patient to experience a return of energy and activity that can be used in resolving life problems.

■ DURATION OF TREATMENT AND TERMINATION

There is overall agreement in the brief-psychotherapy literature that brief psychotherapy should generally be limited to 10– 20 sessions, usually once a week. However, in some cases, up to 40 sessions may be held. If the therapist goes beyond this number, she should be prepared to proceed to a long-term treatment of greater than 40–50 sessions. The duration of treatment is very much related to maintaining the focus. When treatment extends beyond

20 sessions, the therapist may find herself branching into a broad character analysis and losing the focus (Table 13–3).

The termination of brief psychotherapy is very important. Because the treatment is so brief, the ending of treatment is always in the patient's (and the therapist's) mind. In the treatment, the patient experiences the real loss of the treatment and also reexperiences the loss of the transference figure. These losses must be dealt with in a direct and accurate manner for the transference to be experienced as real and central to the patient's present life. The inexperienced therapist may be alert only to the loss of the therapist as a real figure and may miss the opportunity to identify an important transference element from which the patient can both learn and also deeply experience the importance of the childhood figure. The therapist must remember that the loss of this childhood figure may be sad, but it may also be exciting, felt as the freedom to grow and to experience the world of choices and wishes that have long been ignored or inhibited.

Therapists differ on whether an ending date should be specifically chosen when the treatment is begun. Some specify the date and explain at that time their policy on any missed sessions; others merely specify the total number of sessions. Some more senior clinicians leave open the ending time, merely indicating they will meet with the patient for a brief and limited amount of time. Setting a date can enable some patients who are frightened of dependency

---

TABLE 13–3. **Duration and technique of brief psychodynamic psychotherapy**

Duration: 10 to 20 sessions, once a week (can go up to 40)

Technique: focused defense analysis, transference interpretation, and reconstruction

Benign neglect

Termination very important

Ending date or number of sessions generally specified when treatment begins

---

(e.g., obsessional) to enter treatment and can limit the regression of more troublesome cases.

Generally, specifying the ending date relieves the beginning therapist of the task of listening for the resolution of the conflict area and the patient's health-driven wishes to end treatment. Because listening for this resolution is a difficult task, it is often helpful to learn brief psychotherapy with a supervisor and with a specified ending (date or number of sessions). In this way, the beginning, middle, and latter phases of treatment are clearly spelled out for the therapist as well as for the patient. The clinical phenomena that occur in these phases can then be clearly identified. In addition, although specifying the ending date puts the stress on the therapist—typified by the patient's concern "Will anything happen by then!"—it can also relieve the overburdened clinician from the worries of an unending therapy.

■ TECHNIQUES

All the usual techniques of psychodynamic psychotherapy are used in brief therapy: defense analysis, transference interpretation, and reconstruction (Table 13–3). Dreams can also be used with the sophisticated patient in a focal way. Transference interpretations, as always, require tact and education of the patient and should be at a depth the patient can understand. The skilled therapist increasingly differentiates the language used to formulate the transference to himself, or to a colleague, from the language used in talking with the patient. Usually one or two transference interpretations may be made in a 10- or 12-session treatment. With too many interpretations of the transference, the technique becomes trivialized and may be ineffective (11). The patient no longer hears or feels the emotional impact of the relationship as a living of the past in the present.

Very important to the success of the treatment is the use of benign neglect. Many areas of psychodynamic interest appear in the course of a brief treatment. However, the focus must be the central concern for the therapist. Many interesting roads are seen, but the therapist must let them pass without comment.

Keeping in mind the phases of the treatment can help to identify the particular feelings of the patient that are most urgent at any given moment. Early in the treatment, the patient usually experiences a surge of magical expectations about the changes that the therapist will cause to occur. During this phase the therapist need not make many comments. Frequently in the middle phase of the treatment the patient expands his associations to a much wider view than the focal conflict. How this is handled to maintain the focus can be central to whether a brief therapy remains a brief therapy. Resistance will also appear in the middle phase, offering the opportunity to interpret an important defensive style of the patient with its present and past components. Toward the end of the middle phase or the beginning of the termination, a transference theme may become prominent, and it may be able to be interpreted in a direct, supportive, empathic manner that will crystallize the central conflict as it has been patterned by the past and is alive in the present.

Termination always requires dealing with the patient's experience of the loss of the transference figure, the childhood wish for resolution of the past injury, and the real therapist. Not uncommonly, the beginning therapist may feel that he is abandoning the patient. "Is this enough? Does he need more? Should I continue?" The reality of the patient's situation versus the countertransference of the therapist should be considered. More often than not, when the patient has been appropriately selected, the therapist is responding to the transference rather than to a crisis necessitating continuing treatment. Often the last sessions of the treatment provide an opportunity for a transference interpretation related to the particular pattern the patient shows in the wish to hold onto the therapist and the therapy.

If the patient asks for additional sessions, this request must always be heard and listened to but not necessarily agreed to. Whether this is a part of the transference or a new focal area to be worked on must be considered. Certainly the therapist should not use some ideal of termination to disregard a patient in serious difficulty. Some guidelines are helpful: often, if the therapist merely listens and understands, in all its meanings, the patient's wish to hold on to the therapist, the patient feels relieved and can move on. Also, the patient knows the therapist's phone number and can always call if further problems appear. It is helpful for there to be a period in which the patient tries new skills and knowledge, even if a new therapy is undertaken. Such a break in the treatment, with the patient knowing that the therapist is available, can allow the patient's wishes for health to take hold.

■ REFERENCES

1. Luborsky L, Crits-Christoph P: Understanding Transference—The Core Conflictual Relationship Theme (CCRT) Method. New York, Basic Books, 1990
2. Stierlin H: Short-term versus long-term psychotherapy in the light of a general theory of human relationship. Br J Med Psychol 41:357–367, 1968
3. Alexander F: Current views of psychotherapy. Psychiatry 16:113–122, 1953
4. Malan DH: The Frontier of Brief Psychotherapy. New York, Plenum, 1976
5. Sifneos PE: Short-Term Psychotherapy and Emotional Crisis. Cambridge, MA, Harvard University Press, 1972
6. Mann J: Time-Limited Psychotherapy. Cambridge, MA, Harvard University Press, 1973
7. Davanloo H (ed): Basic Principles and Techniques in Short-Term Dynamic Psychotherapy. New York, SP Medical and Scientific Books, 1978
8. Ursano RJ, Hales RE: A review of brief individual therapies. Am J Psychiatry 143:1507–1517, 1986
9. Ursano RJ, Silberman EK: Individual psychotherapies, in The American Psychiatric Press Textbook of Psychiatry. Edited by Talbot JA, Hales RE, Yudofsky SC. Washington, DC, American Psychiatric Press, 1988, pp 855–889

10. Hogland P, Heyerdahl O: The circumscribed focus in intensive brief dynamic psychotherapy. Psychother Psychosom 61:163–170, 1994
11. Hoglend P: Transference interpretations and long-term change after dynamic psychotherapy of brief to moderate length. Am J Psychother 47:494–507, 1993

■ ADDITIONAL READINGS

Balint M, Ornstein PH, Balint E: Focal Psychotherapy: An Example of Applied Psychoanalysis. London, Tavistock, 1972

Bauer GP, Kobos JC: Brief Therapy. Northvale, NJ, Jason Aronson, 1987

Crits-Christoph P, Barber JP (eds): Handbook of Short-Term Dynamic Psychotherapy. New York, Basic Books, 1991

Horowitz M, Marmar C, Krupnick J, et al: Personality Styles and Brief Psychotherapy. New York, Basic Books, 1984

Levenson H: Concise Guide to Time-Limited Psychodynamic Psychotherapy. Washington, DC, American Psychiatric Press, 1997

Malan DH: A Study of Brief Psychotherapy. London, Tavistock, 1963

14

PSYCHOTHERAPY OF BORDERLINE PERSONALITY DISORDER AND OTHER SEVERE CHARACTER PATHOLOGY

Patients with borderline, schizoid, and narcissistic personality disorders constitute a difficult and challenging population for both the beginning therapist and the seasoned clinician. Perhaps with no other group is the therapist so intensely drawn into the emotional immediacy of the patient's world. Because of the intensity and primitiveness of the patient's fundamental anxieties, the frequent fluctuations in the clinical picture, and the rapid and powerful transference feelings about the therapist, conducting therapy with these patients poses an emotional challenge.

■ DIAGNOSIS

The term *borderline personality disorder* is applied to a group of patients with a varied symptom picture. Several different patterns of symptomatology may be present (1). For example, one should consider a borderline diagnosis in a patient with numerous and varied symptoms, including intense free-floating anxiety, many phobias, obsessive rituals, conversion symptoms, or hypochondriasis. These patients predominantly use primitive defense mechanisms and have a particular quality to their internalized object relationships that is evident in their interpersonal relations. The same defenses and object-relationship patterns are mobilized in the transference in psychodynamic psychotherapy (Table 14–1). Much discussed in the last several decades, and very important in the psychotherapy of these patients, is the borderline patient's use of *splitting*. Splitting refers to actively separating the positively toned self and object images from the negatively toned images. This important defense mechanism is part of the reason for the lack of an integrated psychic structure in these patients.

Borderline patients lack a solid and realistic self-image, a healthy self-esteem, and a sense of basic trust in a nurturant mothering figure. Thus, later in adult life, these patients suffer a lack of trust in all relationships, especially intimate ones. Because of the borderline patient's splitting, the clinical picture may markedly change very quickly. For example, the therapist may be idealized at one moment and shortly thereafter devalued, or vice versa. Similarly, the patient's relationships may appear to change in quality in a chaotic manner. For example, the patient may report

TABLE 14–1. **Defense mechanisms in patients with borderline personality disorder**

Defense mechanism	Patient behavior
Splitting	Separation of positive and negative self- and object images
Denial	Deliberately ignoring important realities
Devaluing	Minimizing and dismissing with contempt
Primitive idealization	Exaggerating the power and prestige of another person
Omnipotence	Exaggerating one's own power
Projection	Attributing one's own conflicted impulses to another person
Projective identification	A projection onto someone whom the patient then attempts to control

that former friends and allies have rapidly shifted to become devalued enemies. Dealing with the borderline patient's splitting is a major part of the psychotherapy with these patients.

Other important defenses in the borderline patient include denial, devaluing, primitive idealization, omnipotence, projection, and projective identification. Devaluing and primitive idealization often appear as minimizing or exaggerating the therapist's power and prestige. Omnipotence is seen in a patient's exaggeration of the power of his own thoughts and feelings.

In the treatment setting, projection leads the patient to attribute his own impulses, affects, and other psychic contents to the therapist. Projective identification is a kind of leaky projection. For example, the patient may project his hostility onto the therapist and fearfully anticipate being attacked. At the same time the patient senses that he is somehow connected to and responsible for the hostility in the room. In other words, the patient still identifies with the hostility and feels a need to try to control the therapist's anticipated expression of aggression.

■ CONFLICTS

The major internal conflicts of borderline patients are primitive or *preoedipal* in nature. This leads to sharp contrasts between borderline and neurotic patients. Neurotic patients struggle mainly with the later developmental issues of consolidating gender identity, resolving oedipal longings and rivalries, and establishing a mature ego ideal and conscience (or superego) with firm values. In contrast, borderline patients have never learned to feel safe in the world. Psychoanalytic developmental theorists have described the early history of a future borderline patient as disturbed in the maternal-infant relationship.

The rapprochement phase of separation-individuation is a particularly vulnerable time. It is at this time that the toddler feels secure enough to begin to explore the world on her own, safe in the knowledge that a maternal figure will be available to whom she may return to refuel emotionally. Because of high levels of constitutional aggressiveness and/or overly intense ambivalence and hostility in the mother-infant dyad, these children never feel completely secure. They are never sure their mothers (and later, other figures in their lives) will feel positively toward them and meet their needs.

Arriving at this feeling of *basic trust* or *object constancy* is an essential task of the early phase of personality development. Without the accomplishment of these developmental milestones, the child (and later the adult) is overly vulnerable to feeling *annihilation anxiety*. This overwhelming anxiety transforms the experience of an ordinary life crisis into that of a life-threatening situation. It is this anxiety that the borderline patient is attempting to bind and control with her primitive defenses of splitting, denial, projection, and so forth. It is also this anxiety that will be gradually mobilized and, it is hoped, softened in the unfolding intensive psychotherapy of a borderline adult. The intensity of annihilation anxiety makes the defenses of these patients very tenacious and the treatment and transference-countertransference issues peculiarly intense and challenging.

Borderline patients have their most important difficulties in trusting others, feeling safe, and feeling that they are solid, worthwhile human beings who will make it in the world. However, the clinician should not overlook the fact that these patients also have oedipal-level conflicts similar to those of the more neurotic patient. Earlier developmental issues are carried forward into the later developmental tasks of consolidating gender identity and resolving sexual rivalries (the oedipal conflict) (1). It is as if in the unfolding school of life, no one gets completely flunked and no one gets exempted from passing on to the next grade. We are pushed along, willy-nilly, to confront all the difficult issues, ready or not, carrying along our unresolved conflicts from earlier stages. The unresolved issues fuse with and give a particular form to the anxieties of the later stage.

Thus, a future borderline patient, feeling unsure of mother's predominantly positive investment and feeling fundamentally un-safe in the world, will precociously approach father and experience an intense and premature oedipal conflict. In this way the child tries to resolve gender and genital (or sexual) conflicts and at the same time to obtain the reassuring maternal closeness felt to be inadequate from the maternal figure. Thus, when sexual conflicts are mobilized in the transference in the therapy of a borderline patient, the clinician is inevitably looking at a layering of important anxieties.

Very frequently with these patients, erotic conflicts, attach-ments, and jealousies are more readily and openly discussed than with neurotic patients. This openness occurs because the "higher-level" sexual concern serves in part to mask the deeper and more troubling issues of distrust and poor object constancy.

More recently, theorists have felt that borderline personality disorder is a clinical presentation of patients with an especially vulnerable and fragmenting self. From this perspective, the symp-toms of borderline patients emerge when stabilizing relationships with other people are lost. These relationships on which the indi-vidual with borderline personality disorder depends are called *selfobject* bonds. The disruption of these stabilizing bonds leads to the rage and chaotic behavior so often described in borderline patients. From this vantage point, borderline personality disorder represents a particularly severe form of self disorder.

Traditionally, borderline personality disorder has been seen as especially difficult to treat; now, data support psychodynamic psychotherapy as perhaps the treatment of choice for this group of patients. Experience with these patients has shown that they can often gradually improve in treatment to the more cohesive and less labile level of functioning of the narcissistic personality.

■ BEGINNING PSYCHOTHERAPY

On commencing psychotherapy with borderline patients, the thera-pist needs to keep several important issues in mind to diagnose and control dangerous acting out. Acting out may be part of the presenting problems or may erupt early in treatment because of the rapidity of intense transference developments. A good guide for judging the potential for rage and self-destructiveness is the patient's history, especially the history of the events that triggered past hospitalizations, suicide attempts, and other regressions.

The clinician must be prepared to manage the patient's regressions and self-destructiveness (Table 14–2). The therapist may make use of an auxiliary physician to handle any medications needed and a social worker to monitor and help structure daily living. It may also help to have access to an acute inpatient psychiatric service, an emergency room psychiatric service, and continuous-call coverage, particularly for weekends and vacations. In addition, the therapist needs to process intellectually, in a more deliberate manner than with more intact patients, the life events and communications of a borderline patient. These patients may often indicate the beginning of a suicidal or otherwise dangerous

---

TABLE 14–2. **Principles of treatment of patients with borderline personality disorder and other severe character pathology**

Manage destructive acting out through

    Hospitalization.

    Emergency room visits.

    Medication.

    Environmental structuring.

    Physician availability.

Use both intellectual and emotional understanding of the patients' communications.

Interpret negative transference and reality distortions quickly and tactfully.

Interpret primitive defenses (see Table 14–1).

Contain and understand countertransference reactions.

---

emotional constellation in an oblique and unemotional way because of their lack of trust and their denial of painful affects.

The therapist's affective and intellectual stance should be calm emotional availability based on concern, interest, and neutrality. Suggestion and manipulation should be avoided. Frequently the ready availability of historic material tempts the therapist to make premature interpretations. The therapist, in fact, should proceed slowly and cautiously with interpretations that link current problems with developmental issues in the patient's early life. It is important to explore the negative transference in the here and now. The positive transference is used to further the treatment and is not interpreted. In addition, the patient's perceptions are clarified, acting out is blocked, and primitive defenses are carefully interpreted.

■ PSYCHOTHERAPEUTIC WORK WITH THE BORDERLINE PATIENT'S DEFENSES

Work with the borderline patient's primitive defenses occupies a major portion of the psychotherapy of borderline patients. Splitting is evident in the treatment as the borderline patient alternates between the positive and negative self and object images in a sequential fashion instead of experiencing mixed feelings, or ambivalence, in a given moment. Thus, it becomes important to bear in mind that when a patient's attitude and affect toward a person or a given issue seem utterly different from those on a previous day or week, the shift is probably a result of splitting rather than of genuine change, as is seen in the following example:

> A beautiful 25-year-old married woman presented for treatment with symptoms related to an unresolved intense dependency on her dying mother, who resided in another country. The patient had long suffered gastrointestinal symptoms and anxiety, and these were now ex-

acerbated by the pressure she felt from her female thesis advisor. She described this woman as a rigid, critical, competitive "witch," older and, by implication, envious of the patient's beauty and other gifts. The patient had a similarly negative opinion of her mother-in-law and of several women acquaintances. In therapy she quickly idealized the therapist as a warm and intelligent guiding figure, but this image was abruptly shattered when she realized the therapist would charge her for missed appointments that had not been filled during the patient's visits home to her native country. At moments of such disillusionment the patient described the therapist as cold, exploitative, dishonest, and unaffectionate. Under the pressure of these attacks, the therapist experienced the patient as critical, demanding, contemptuous, and intolerant, much like the hated thesis advisor and mother-in-law.

After the mother's death, the patient's oscillation between positive and negative experiences of the therapist and of important others in the patient's life intensified. The patient was alternately deeply grateful for extra therapy sessions and suspicious that the therapist intended to cheat her financially. She spent weeks at a time alternating between loving and feeling protective toward her widowed father and hating him and wishing him dead as he began to date another woman.

Over many months, while the patient was at times filled with hatred of the therapist and the father, the therapist interpreted the patient's splitting by reminding her of her more positive feelings and of the difficulty she had in tolerating her own ambivalence. Eventually, the therapist and the father were seen more ambivalently and as human—neither all good nor all evil. Only then was the patient able to experience and share her intense grief over her mother's death. After several years of mending the split between her hatred and her love, it was possible to trace the patient's hostility to her disavowed competition with and rage at her all-protecting, "saintly" mother.

In contrast to working with better-integrated patients, the therapist treating a borderline patient must do most of the work of assembling, organizing, and remembering the disparate images and affective states of the patient in order to integrate them. Only then is it possible to present the feelings back to the patient as various facets of the same conflict that had been defensively separated and split apart.

In addition to clarifying and interpreting the defensive use of splitting, the therapist confronts and interprets the other typical defenses of the borderline personality disorder (Table 14–1). The following two examples illustrate these points:

Case 1. An alcoholic patient emerged, over the course of therapy, from a chaotic marriage in which she had played a masochistic and submissive role with an immature and irresponsible husband. After the marital breakup she found herself shouldering greatly increased financial responsibility, working full time, and caring for her home and her young children alone. During many sessions the patient would report and associate to her anxiety, helplessness, and resentment as she assumed increasingly autonomous functioning. However, the therapist noted that for a number of weeks the patient had not mentioned her drinking, which at times had reached dangerous levels. When the therapist drew this to the patient's attention, confronting the patient's denial and eliciting this serious and neglected material, the patient burst into tears and acknowledged her terror that the alcohol would kill her. By denying her drinking, she had also been denying the intensity of her panic.

Case 2. A 53-year-old woman had been in intensive treatment for several years and had slowly emerged from her isolation and suicidal preoccupation. After weeks of feeling a new gratitude and affection for the therapist, she suddenly relapsed. One morning when the therapist was 11 minutes late for their appointment, the patient was sullen, bitter, and quietly enraged. By insisting gently and firmly that the patient describe her feelings, the therapist was able to elicit the patient's nearly paranoid description of the therapist as haughty, aloof, rigid, superior, and contemptuous of the patient's own busy professional schedule. The therapist then asked the patient if this description in fact corresponded with the years of experience the patient had had with her.

Puzzled, the patient acknowledged it did not, but it did match the way she had at times experienced her mother. Most important, it matched the way the patient herself often felt toward her own employees. The patient was also able to acknowledge how anxiety-provoking and disorienting it had been to feel positively about the therapist in the recent sessions.

In this last vignette several important issues encountered in the therapy of borderline patients are illustrated:

- The patient's use of projective identification is evident. A haughty, harsh, and punitive aspect of herself was projected onto the therapist, but the patient still felt anxiously connected to this part of her and fearful of the hostility she expected to be directed at her.
- The vignette shows the importance of confronting and exploring negative transference quickly, because it can escalate, disrupt the therapeutic alliance, and threaten the continuity of the treatment.

- The regression in the transference in this case is very typical following a new closeness with and appreciation for the therapist, especially by previously aloof and hostile patients. As the patient explained, her emotional isolation and distrust were painful but familiar, and she was terrified of losing herself in a relationship of trust and love.
- The vignette also illustrates the importance of clarifying the patient's perceptions, especially when they are at serious variance with reality (2). In this case, if the transference reaction had been permitted to persist unchallenged, it might have become a *transference psychosis,* a delusional conviction about the therapist coupled with a loss of reality testing. In borderline, as opposed to psychotic, patients, a transference psychosis is generally confined to the therapy sessions and is not accompanied by a disorganization outside the therapeutic hours. However, it is an ominous development that requires immediate and careful attention.

Borderline patients frequently do not understand the words a therapist uses. The families of borderline patients use words to manipulate or to mean the opposite of their manifest content. This experience of the therapist's spoken words has important implications for technique, especially at moments of intense transference reactions. As in the previous vignette, it is doubly important with these patients not to reassure or to appear to dismiss fears about the therapist's intentions. Frequently, in the heat of a negative transference, actions speak louder than words. For example, it may help, paradoxically, to offer an extra session to a hostile, accusing, and fearful patient more than to declare one's benevolent intentions. The therapist, by repeating the patient's charges against her in a calm and nondefensive tone of voice, can go a long way toward reality testing her "evil" intent while inviting exploration and indicating acceptance and valuing of the emotional communication.

Because of the intensity of their conflicts and the fragility of their egos, many borderline patients are action oriented and can quickly become negative and resistant, turning a deaf ear to the therapist. One patient was taken aback by an interpretation she later acknowledged to be highly accurate. However, her first reaction was a hostile, "What does that mean?" Another patient, in a similar situation, commented, "I've heard only half of what you said, and I feel like I've been badgered all morning." One needs to proceed gently and tactfully and also to bear in mind that negative feelings are not avoidable with this group of patients.

■ COUNTERTRANSFERENCE

How to use the transference-countertransference relatedness with borderline patients is one of the most difficult, emotionally draining, and potentially rewarding skills for a therapist to learn. Understanding this interplay is often especially difficult for the young clinician, who may hear a patient's typical devaluing of the therapist's skill as an accurate reflection of his inexperience. The therapist's helpless feelings in this setting can lead to harmful effects on the relationship.

The therapist is helped by maintaining the following perspectives and attitudes (Table 14–3):

Table 14–3.   **Helpful therapeutic attitudes in the treatment of patients with borderline personality disorder**

Remember that the patient's experience of the therapist derives for the most part from the past.

Maintain the sense of oneself as a concerned physician.

Do not take the patient's negative feelings personally.

Adopt an attitude of using every session to promote progress and understanding.

Honestly recognize one's own intense rage and hatred.

- "A little of what the patient attributes to me is likely to be true, but nonetheless the importance of the patient's way of experiencing me relates to the patient's inner conflicts." All people have similar human concerns, and in trying to integrate, for example, the felt harshness of a parent, a patient may well succeed in eliciting for a time some countertransference harshness from the therapist.

- "In the face of a patient's accusations of my hostility or indifference, I shall not lose my grip on the conviction that I am fundamentally a responsible and concerned physician, interested in the patient's welfare, despite my occasionally intense countertransference irritation."

- "I shall adopt an attitude of accepting a patient's negative feelings with interest and concern and with an eye to interpreting these feelings without taking them personally." Again, at times, repeating the accusations calmly with a nondefensive tone and an exploratory intent will go a long way toward defusing hostility.

- "I shall adopt an attitude of using every session to promote progress and understanding. I shall be patient over the long haul about the slow pace with which many borderline patients progress." However, drifting through many sessions, lulled by a borderline patient's intense defenses without ever confronting them, will destroy the sense of meaningfulness of the therapy and lead to a stalemate (3).

- "I shall try to honestly recognize periods of intense rage and hatred that I may feel toward my patient and to understand the transference feelings that elicit my reaction." If a therapist buries these affects because they affront his self-image as a concerned physician, treatment disruption or a suicide attempt may result (4).

Ultimately, the goal with borderline patients is to work steadily toward a greater sense of safety and greater trust and openness with the therapist. The increased security and trust will then generalize to the patient's life in the world and to other relationships. Border-line patients are inevitably very dependent, although their powerful defenses often mask this trait. As with the case example in the previous section, the experience in therapy of trust and dependence is both a necessary and a highly feared development. It should be approached slowly, recognizing that it flowers haltingly. With an acceptance and softening of their dependence left over from early childhood, borderline patients experience an increase in self-reliance and self-esteem.

■ NARCISSISTIC AND SCHIZOID PATIENTS

Both narcissistic and schizoid patients are in many ways similar to the borderline patient in the nature of their underlying anxieties and in the defense mechanisms they employ. Narcissistic patients, however, tend to have a more stable personal history than do borderline patients, especially in their work history. A narcissistic patient's personal history, however, like the borderline patient's, will show a characteristic lack of trusting intimacy. Therapy with a narcissistic patient tends to focus on a narrower range of issues than does therapy with a borderline patient. There is less of a propensity for annihilation anxiety and more of a concern with fragile self-esteem. Narcissistic patients establish typical transference ways of relating. One group may appear grandiose and demanding of constant admiration from the therapist, whose separate personality they do not seem to recognize. Another group will intensely idealize the therapist, with whose felt superiority they long to identify.

These two forms of transference, called *mirroring* and *idealizing* transferences, are characteristic of narcissistic personality disorder (5). Patients with this disorder tend to treat the therapist as an extension of themselves, much as a very young child assumes a right to his mother's attention with no concern for her separate needs. In general, interpretations are directed toward the patient's lack of self-esteem and longing for parental figures to admire, praise, instruct, model, and accurately reflect the patient's personality. With treatment and consolidation of self-esteem, these patients experience a greater capacity for self-regulation, emotional depth, and deeper intimacy. The countertransference difficulties tend to be the therapist's discomfort at being viewed as an extension of the patient and the therapist's difficulty in withstanding and interpreting the demands for admiration and benevolent protection.

Because of work with narcissistic patients, the importance of the cohesiveness of the self and self-esteem in motivating human development has become clearer. From this vantage point, drives and oedipal conflicts are seen as secondary to the absence or loss of normal selfobject ties and vulnerabilities in the cohesiveness of the self.

Schizoid patients are like quiet borderline patients. Generally, they have a less chaotic personal history but share with the borderline patient a lack of basic trust. They are less flamboyant, emotionally labile, and action-oriented than borderline patients. Therapists can be fooled by schizoid patients' seeming calm and can underestimate the depth of their despair, which may not be communicated directly because of a schizoid patient's lack of trust. With these patients in particular, one must be intellectually, as well as emotionally, aware of events in the patients' lives that could trigger suicidal feeling, such as job loss or loss of even a "casual" friend or acquaintance. The goal of treatment with schizoid patients is to improve the capacity for emotional contact, trust, and enhanced self-esteem.

■ CONCLUSIONS

Psychotherapy with borderline, narcissistic, and schizoid patients is arduous and potentially rewarding work. Especially with this fragile group, the therapist needs to understand intellectually, as well as emotionally, the patient's communications. This understanding is important to the therapist's ability to monitor the patient's day-to-day safety and eventually to integrate the patient's split-apart positive and negative self- and object images. It is important to address the patient's splitting, denial, negative transference, reality distortions, and primitive defenses. Tact, empathy, and careful timing are crucial; however, negative transference is never completely avoidable. Countertransference feelings are often intense and difficult to contain. However, tolerating and examining these reactions are powerful therapeutic tools. Ultimately, what is therapeutic for these patients is the therapist's capacity to understand, contain, integrate, and reflect back the patients' intense and painful feelings.

■ REFERENCES

1. Kernberg OF: Borderline Conditions and Pathological Narcissism. New York, Jason Aronson, 1975
2. Volkan V: Six Steps in the Treatment of Borderline Personality Organization. Northvale, NJ, Jason Aronson, 1987
3. Kernberg OF: Structural change and its impediments, in Borderline Personality Disorders. Edited by Hartocollis P. New York, International Universities Press, 1977, pp 275–306
4. Buie D, Maltsberger JT: Countertransference hate in the treatment of suicidal patients. Arch Gen Psychiatry 30:625–633, 1974
5. Kohut H: The Analysis of the Self. New York, International Universities Press, 1971

■ ADDITIONAL READINGS

Adler G: The borderline-narcissistic personality disorder continuum. Am J Psychiatry 138:40–50,1981
Chatham P: Treatment of the Borderline Personality. Northvale, NJ, Jason Aronson, 1985
Kohut H: The Restoration of the Self. New York, International Universities Press, 1977
Kohut H: How Does Analysis Cure? Chicago, The University of Chicago Press, 1984
Lichtenberg J: Psychoanalysis and Motivation. Hillsdale, NJ, Analytic Press, 1989

Stolorow RR, Branscraft G, Atwood G: Treatment of borderline states, in Psychoanalytic Treatment: An Intersubjective Approach. Hillsdale, NJ, Analytic Press, 1987, pp 110–130

15

SUPPORTIVE PSYCHOTHERAPY

Supportive psychotherapy is the most often used form of psychotherapy in clinical practice. Despite this, little has been written about this modality, and even less systematic research has been done on it. Much of the basic understanding of the effects of supportive psychotherapy as well as the techniques involved derives from the psychoanalytic perspective on mental functioning (1–3). Supportive psychotherapy is very demanding of the skills of the therapist. It requires an understanding of the role of developmental history in the formation of the patient's disease and a thorough understanding of the effects of the therapeutic alliance and transference on the doctor-patient relationship. Because the relationship with the patient is less structured and therefore more subject to rapid, unexpected changes, supportive psychotherapy can be a very difficult form of treatment to sustain over the very long duration frequently required.

Supportive psychotherapy is defined by its goals and techniques. In contrast to the other psychoanalytic psychotherapies, which are change oriented, supportive psychotherapy aims to help the patient reestablish his previous best level of functioning, given the limitations of illness, ability, biological givens, and life circumstances (Table 15–1). The difference between supportive psychotherapy and other psychotherapies has been likened to the difference between the treatment for viral infection and the treatment for bacterial infection. In general, the treatment of viral infection is supportive, giving the assistance needed to sustain the patient and facilitate the natural healing in an environment that

TABLE 15–1.	Goal selection and duration of supportive psychotherapy

Goal

Maintain or reestablish usual level of functioning.

Selection

Patient is very healthy but with severe stressor, or patient is severely or chronically ill with ego deficits.

Patient is able to recognize safety and develop trust.

Duration

Treatment can last days to years.

does not contribute added risk. In contrast, bacterial infections are specifically treated with antibiotic agents to remove the cause of the disease (4). In fact, all treatments—the psychotherapies and psychoanalysis in particular—include supportive elements (2). So this distinction is more one of degree than of an absolute, as it may at first appear.

■ SELECTION OF PATIENTS

Patients for supportive psychotherapy fall into two categories: 1) very healthy individuals who are well adapted but have become impaired because of overwhelming life events, and 2) individuals who have serious psychiatric illness or who are chronically disturbed and have significant deficits in ego functioning (Table 15–1). The very healthy patient has been momentarily overwhelmed and does not lack crucial mental functions to cope, once the balance of mental functioning and the reserves of mental energy are restored. Most patients who have been exposed to true traumatic events (e.g., war, earthquakes, disasters caused by people, motor vehicle accidents) fall into this first category and will recover their normal functioning with supportive treatment. In contrast, the second and more typical patient has chronic difficulties and lacks certain capacities necessary for benefiting from change-oriented therapies.

The typical patient suffers from poor reality testing, poor impulse control, limited interpersonal relations, constricted or overwhelming affect, and externalization of conflicts. Candidates for supportive psychotherapy do not experience significant relief by only understanding—either because they do not think psychologically or because they do not apply or generalize the knowledge, once gained. Frequently they have primitive defenses such as splitting, projective identification, and denial, which cause them to experience the world as chronically threatening and without much safety. Thus, the therapeutic alliance may be difficult to sustain; the therapist may need to use active intervention to demonstrate the concern and safety of the therapeutic relationship. Frequently the patient's conflicts and behaviors are chronic and elicit from the environment reciprocal self-fulfilling actions. The masochistic patient finds sadistic attack, the angry help-seeking patient finds rejection, and the borderline and histrionic patient finds exploitation (5). Because of this complex interpersonal field, the recognition and management of transference and countertransference are central to effective supportive psychotherapy.

Despite these areas of relative weakness, the patient must show an ability to develop trust in an interpersonal relationship. Although the patient may not be able to sustain a sense of safety in thought and fantasy, she must be able to recognize safety and reality when explained and demonstrated in action over time. A stable, even though limited, work and interpersonal life is a good prognostic sign. The patient who had some positive experiences with a parent or older sibling who was experienced as benign, or at least as doing the best he could, frequently does better in this form of psychotherapy.

The clinician is at times helped by remembering that there are alternative interventions to supportive psychotherapy for the patient with severe ego deficits. Counseling, rehabilitative services, and environmental manipulation are effective interventions when supportive psychotherapy is not indicated. In addition, medication, of course, can be very effective. Without psychotherapy, however, medication compliance and the interpersonal and social aspects of illness will not generally improve under chronic conditions. These areas can be addressed through the psychotherapeutic work.

■ TECHNIQUES

An in-depth understanding of the patient's developmental history and defense mechanisms is as important to supportive psychotherapy as it is to the other psychoanalytically oriented psychotherapies. Only with this knowledge can the therapist accurately assess the frequently changing therapeutic alliance, know how and where to strengthen the patient's defenses, and understand when and how to address the transference. These are the central aspects of providing support, a very difficult concept to understand and a difficult technical skill to master.

Developing and maintaining a good working relationship with the patient is the first priority of supportive psychotherapy. The therapist's regular and predictable availability forms the basis of the therapeutic relationship and of a new experience in the patient's life (Table 15–2). Because the work and relationship in supportive psychotherapy are not built on the patient's observing and reporting moment-to-moment feeling states in the therapy or on talking about feelings about the therapist, as in other forms of psychodynamic psychotherapy, the relationship with the doctor is different. The doctor's relationship to the patient is more one of guide and mentor.

The working relationship and the trust and experience of safety it requires are the result of the therapist's recognition of the complex feeling states of the patient at any given moment. When the patient is using projection and describing the dangers all around, the knowledgeable therapist understands the growing aggression in the patient and looks for what may be the unfulfilled wish or the activation of a destructive desire as an identification with a hated

---

TABLE 15–2.   **Techniques of supportive psychotherapy**

Know the patient's defenses and developmental conflicts.

Establish and maintain the therapeutic alliance.

Provide a holding environment.

Organize the patient's cognitions ("lending the therapist's ego").

Constantly attend to the state of the transference.

Express in modulated form the patient's affects.

Explore alternative actions.

Use interpretation sparingly and supportively.

Use medication and explore compliance.

---

parent. Thus, using the psychodynamic understanding of the patient's life, the therapist can choose to ask, "What are your plans for looking for your next job?"or to express in modulated form the patient's anger, "You felt your boss's anger and must wish you could express yours." The therapist's ability to provide support is based on the clinician's understanding of the patient's present conflict, of the state of the patient's defenses, and of the transference. With this knowledge the therapist can intervene to express the feelings of the patient in a modulated manner, recognize the patient's successes, and provide a *holding environment* in which delay and inhibited action will relieve the patient's downhill spiral.

The often stated idea that the therapist gives advice is generally a misunderstanding of what actually occurs in good psychotherapy. The patient in supportive psychotherapy is no less likely to experience ambivalence and reject advice than anyone else. Nor is the therapist any wiser in supportive psychotherapy than in other psychotherapies! It is more accurate to describe the actions of the therapist as organizing and exploring alternatives (6).

When the clinician tells the patient to take a cab to come in and see her, she is providing momentary organization for the patient's internal and external life in a way similar to a hospitalization. This is often called "lending the patient the therapist's ego." However, when the patient has a complex decision to make, such as a divorce, remarriage, or change of job, the therapist usually helps the most and maintains the therapeutic alliance best by exploring all the options and the advantages and disadvantages of each with the patient.

In fact, this technique is not greatly different from the work of psychoanalytic psychotherapy. However, in psychoanalytic psychotherapy this part is usually carried out by the patient alone after identifying the neurotic element that is causing a blind spot. In supportive psychotherapy, the therapist both helps the patient see why he may be overlooking an area—"I wonder if you haven't mentioned the idea of not going home to your mother's because of the feeling that you don't want to disappoint her? We know how bad that makes you feel"—and then explores the options after they are all spelled out—"Well, yes, not going would feel bad for you when you are feeling it is a disappointment to her; but you would also feel more in control of your job and of the decisions about what your family needs."

The therapist's ability to recognize and respect the patient's alternating desires for independence and refueling can be a source of countertransference frustration for the therapist. The patient is likely to respond to a success with a need to retreat to the therapist's positive regard and protection. This often-repeated scenario demands an understanding therapist who can see this drama in its historical context and not experience it as a personal blow. After many repetitions, the therapist may find a way to talk with the patient about this alternating movement without the patient's feeling that the therapist is rejecting or frustrated by the patient's neediness.

Although interpretation is not the mainstay of supportive psychotherapy, it is not absent in this treatment (Table 15–3). However, interpretations in supportive psychotherapy differ in how they are given, in their frequency, and in the preliminary work required to ensure that the patient can hear them as supportive and useful (7). Interpretations are more often given in times of low

TABLE 15–3. **Use of interpretation in supportive psychotherapy**

Use interpretation sparingly.

Prepare the patient.

Provide reassurance at the same time as interpretation.

Give the patient room to reject the interpretation.

Give the patient aid in working through reactions to interpretation.

emotional intensity, with the patient alert to the idea that an interpretation will soon be given and with the goal of decreasing the patient's anxiety. In addition, the patient may explicitly be given more room to reject the interpretation ("Maybe you had some feeling of . . ."). The therapist does not remain silent after the interpretation but specifically stays vocally and affectively available to the patient to aid in processing the new material.

Medication can be an important aspect of supportive psychotherapy. The exploration of the patient's feelings and thoughts about any changes in medications can aid compliance. When the patient feels her concerns have been heard, she is more likely to feel safe. Neurotic or psychotic conflict areas that may lead to stopping medication (e.g., "This medication is what my mother used to take!") should be explored and supportively interpreted, and accurate information should be given. At times, the choice of an alternative medication can also avoid possible noncompliance, and dynamic understanding of the problem can help in the selection of the medication.

■ **REFERENCES**

1. Buckley P: Supportive psychotherapy: a neglected treatment. Psychiatric Annals 16:515–521, 1986
2. Jonghe F De, Rijnierse P, Janssen R: Psychoanalytic supportive psychotherapy. J Am Psychoanal Assoc 42:421–446, 1994

3. Rockland LH. A review of supportive psychotherapy 1986–1992. Hosp Community Psychiatry 44:1053–1060, 1993

4. Ursano RJ, Silberman EK: Psychoanalysis, psychoanalytic psychotherapy, and supportive psychotherapy, in The American Psychiatric Press Textbook of Psychiatry, 2nd Edition. Edited by Hales RE, Yudofsky SC, Talbot JA. Washington, DC, American Psychiatric Press, 1994, pp 1035–1060

5. Werman DS: The Practice of Supportive Psychotherapy. New York, Brunner/Mazel, 1984

6. Winston A, Pinsker H, McCullough L: A review of supportive psychotherapy. Hosp Community Psychiatry 37:1105–1114, 1986

7. Pine F: Supportive psychotherapy: a psychoanalytic perspective. Psychiatric Annals 16:526–534, 1986

■ ADDITIONAL READINGS

Dewald PA: Principles of supportive psychotherapy. Am J Psychiatry 48:505–518, 1994

Kahana RJ, Bibring GL: Personality types in medical management, in Psychiatry and Medical Practice in a General Hospital. Edited by Zinberg NF. New York, International Universities Press, 1964, pp 108–123

Kernberg OF: Supportive psychotherapy, in Severe Personality Disorders: Psychotherapeutic Strategies. New Haven, CT, Yale University Press, 1984, pp 147–164

Novalis PN, Rojcewicz SJ Jr, Peele R: Clinical Manual of Supportive Psychotherapy. Washington, DC, American Psychiatric Press, 1993

Wallace ER: Supportive psychotherapy, in Dynamic Psychiatry in Theory and Practice. Philadelphia, PA, Lea & Febiger, 1983, pp 344–371

APPENDIX:
A BRIEF HISTORY OF
PSYCHODYNAMIC
PSYCHOTHERAPY

Psychodynamic psychotherapy is more than a hundred years old (Table App–1). Among its important precursors are the contributions of Charcot and his student Janet. Charcot worked with hysterical patients in Paris and recognized the psychological origins of hysteria, distinguishing it from neurological disease. Charcot felt that the vulnerability to hysteria was physical and constitutional. Janet also considered hysteria psychogenic but developed a psychodynamic theory to explain its origin. For the treatment of these patients, he described a type of psychotherapy which would restore psychological equilibrium and relieve the effect of subconscious fixed ideas.

The Freudian era began with the treatment of Bertha Pappenheim by Freud's colleague, Josef Breuer. The treatment of the woman in this case, "Anna O," was documented by Freud and Breuer in "Studies On Hysteria" (1, 2) in 1895. The treatment focused on the recovery through hypnosis of individual traumatic memories that seemed connected to Pappenheim's many symptoms. During this early period, Freud continued to use hypnosis with his patients. His initial clinical theory was based on the *abreaction* of previously unexpressed affects (feelings) associated with past traumatic events, which were recalled during hypnosis.

Hearing many stories of childhood seduction from his patients,

TABLE APP–1.	History of psychodynamic psychotherapy	
Era	Contributor	Contribution
1889	Charcot	Psychogenic origin of hysteria
1901	Janet	A kind of dynamic psychotherapy "Subconscious fixed ideas"
1895	Breuer	Treatment of Bertha Pappenheim with hypnosis to abreact traumatic memories to relieve symptoms
1900–1923	Sigmund Freud	Theory of instincts in conflict leading to symptoms
		Technique of free association
		Theories of the unconscious, repression, transference, and resistance
1936–1965	Anna Freud	Elaboration of defense mechanisms
		Introduction of play therapy for children
1929–1945	Melanie Klein	Psychotherapy with children
		Therapeutic focus on envy and aggression
1940	Fairbairn	Focus on early relationships with caregivers
		Object relations theory
1966–present	Kernberg	Object relations theorist
		Focus on "splitting" and on treatment of severe personality disorders
1971–1981	Kohut	Self psychology
		Focus on self-cohesion and self-esteem
1960s–present	Infant researchers	Documentation and greater awareness of infant development
1960s–present	Brief psychotherapy research and treatment	Empirical study of psychodynamic psychotherapy
		Techniques to enhance brief psychodynamic psychotherapy
1970s–present	Trauma research	Confirmation of the importance of abuse and trauma in psychiatric disorders
		Focus on the psychotherapy of trauma patients

Freud at first took these accounts literally. Later he decided that many of these stories were based on fantasy and were influenced by the child's psychosexual instinctual development. This, Freud's second theory, was elaborated in 1905 in the "Three Essays On Sexuality" (3). In these essays and subsequent writings, Freud outlined the way children learned about the world through the lenses of the oral, anal, and genital stages of early childhood. These stages of development, and their associated impulses, could lead to conflicts due to the reactions of caregivers, resulting repression, and subsequent symptoms.

Freud placed special emphasis on the formative nature of the powerful issues around the *oedipal conflict,* the child's longing for the parent of the opposite sex and the feared opposition from the parent of the same sex, rooted in the growth of the child away from early nurturing figures and to more mature attachments. With the introduction of the concept of conflict, Freud's clinical approach shifted from the use of hypnosis and abreaction to the search for and interpretation of repressed infantile wishes (particularly those related to bodily impulses). Freud's technique shifted to *free association:* the patient on the couch was instructed to talk in an uncensored manner, telling all the thoughts that came to mind.

As Freud's experience with his patients increased, he noticed factors in his patients that resisted the work of analysis and the uncovering of conflicts. These mental functions that resisted the work of recovering memories were called *defense mechanisms.* With this discovery, he expanded his theory to the well-known tripartite model of mental functions, composed of three functional parts: the ego (rational thought that deals with external reality), the superego (internalized prohibitions and ideals), and the id (the reservoir of instinctual urges and conflicted impulses and wishes). Anna Freud expanded on her father's understanding of the forces keeping conflicts unconscious when she elaborated on the defense mechanisms in her *The Ego and the Mechanisms of Defense* (4) in 1936.

After Freud, a variety of clinicians continued to observe and describe clinical phenomena in greater depth and breadth and to develop newer techniques for a widening range of clinical problems.

Anna Freud developed play therapy for engaging young children in psychodynamic treatment. In psychodynamic play therapy, child patients enact conflicts in the course of play, which are interpreted by the therapist in a manner analogous to the analyst's interpretation of an adult patient's transference and resistances.

Melanie Klein, another innovative clinician and theoretician of childhood psychopathology, contributed her observations of early infantile aggression and envy and advocated a new approach that led to earlier recognition and interpretation of aggression. Both Klein and W. Ronald D. Fairbairn contributed to our awareness of the importance of the child's relationships with caregivers to later adult personality and behavior. Klein and Fairbairn were early contributors to object relations clinical theory, which stresses how early childhood relationships form the templates for later interpersonal patterns. These early relationships are internalized and reactivated later in a patient's life, including the transference in psychodynamic treatment.

Otto Kernberg, perhaps the foremost American object relations theorist, extended this clinical theory to work with borderline patients and others with severe personality disorders. He drew special attention to the primitive defense of *splitting,* which characterizes the psyche of borderline patients and which became an important focus of therapists' work with these patients.

Paula Heimann and Heinrich Racker contributed an awareness of the clinically useful nature of countertransference phenomena, the emotional reactions of the therapist to the patient's transferences. These clinicians emphasized that it was the examination of the patient's transference and the therapist's countertransference together that provided vital information about a patient's internalized images of early relationships.

Heinz Kohut further expanded both theory and the technical approach to patients with narcissistic personality disorders and patients with disorders of the self. In Kohut's experience and thinking, self-esteem and the experience of self-cohesiveness versus fragmentation were the most important clinical issues. In his system of thought, all other clinical issues are byproducts of disturbances of the self system. His contributions have led to psychotherapy's increased attention to empathy as a clinical tool and to the therapist's attending to the patient's sense of safety and self-cohesiveness as important feelings that tell a story of early childhood experiences.

Infant researchers and clinicians, such as Emde, Greenspan, Mahler, and Stern, have contributed a wealth of new experimental data and scientifically documented developmental milestones that have both confirmed and at times challenged older psychoanalytic assumptions about normal development (5). It is development that provides the patterning of mental function and conflicts that are the focus of psychodynamic attention. Among the many contributions these workers made to psychotherapy is a new awareness of the wide range of the infant's inborn sensitivities and given temperaments. Their work has brought attention to the process of development and personality formation—a much more subtle interweaving of constitutional givens and the interpersonal environment than was appreciated initially by Freud.

Recent work by researchers on the impact of trauma and on brief psychodynamic psychotherapy has broadened both our clinical understanding and our therapeutic technique for many patients. Although Freud had discarded the seduction theory of neurosis, experts on trauma have more recently confirmed the importance of real traumatic events in the histories of patients with borderline and multiple personality disorders and their frequency in our everyday lives. In addition, work with patients traumatized both as children and as adults has led to new awareness of the need for psychotherapy for these patients. Janus Bullman, Judith Herman, Mardi Horowitz, Richard Kluft, Jacob Lindy, Robert Pynoos, Arieh Shalev, Lenore Terr, Robert Ursano, Bessel van der Kolk, and Lars Weisæth have made important contributions to the understanding of the theory and psychodynamics and treatment of these disorders (5, 6). Recent work on brief psychodynamic psychotherapy by Crits-Christoph, Davanloo, Luborsky, Malan, Mann, Sifneos, and Strupp have highlighted empirical work on both the process and the outcome of psychodynamic psychotherapy. These individuals have developed important empirical investigations of outcome that can shed light on the psychodynamic process and the critical question of which patient for which treatment.

Although spanning a scant hundred years since Janet and Freud, the history of dynamic psychotherapy has encompassed an accelerating expansion of information and clinical expertise. What began as "Studies on Hysteria" has broadened into the investigation and treatment of emotional illness throughout the human life cycle. Psychodynamic psychotherapy explores the subtleties of the effect of the mind-body connection and the constitutional-experiential interface throughout the life cycle on behavior and our internal as well as interpersonal lives. It is the patterns of early childhood—laid down on the basis of our biological givens, our early familial experiences, and our interpersonal world—that form the lenses through which we view the world throughout our lives and that give meaning to our adult experiences. Psychodynamic psychotherapy looks to change the present patterns of behavior through understanding the relationship of present symptomatic behaviors to past experiences that have provided the templates for these behaviors and for adult cognitive and emotional perception.

■ REFERENCES

1. Freud S: Studies on Hysteria (1895), in The Standard Edition of the Complete Psychological Works of Sigmund Freud, Vol 2. Translated and edited by Strachey, J. London, Hogarth Press, 1955
2. Wallerstein RS: Psychoanalysis and psychotherapy: an historical perspective. Int J Psychoanal 70:563–591, 1989
3. Freud S: Three Essays on Sexuality (1905), in The Standard Edition of the Complete Psychological Works of Sigmund Freud, Vol 7. Translated and edited by Strachey J. London, Hogarth Press, 1953

4. Freud A: The Ego and the Mechanisms of Defense, Revised Edition. New York, International Universities Press, 1966

5. Nersessian E, Kopf RG: Textbook of Psychoanalysis. Washington, DC, American Psychiatric Press, 1996

6. Ursano RJ, McCaughy B, Fullerton CS (eds): Individual and Community Responses to Trauma and Disaster: The Structure of Human Chaos. Cambridge, UK, Cambridge University Press, 1994

■ ADDITIONAL READINGS

Traditional Classics

Freud A: Normality and Pathology in Childhood: Assessments of Development. New York, International Universities Press. 1965

Freud S: Beyond the Pleasure Principle (1920), in The Standard Edition of the Complete Psychological Works of Sigmund Freud, Vol 18. Translated and edited by Strachey J. London, Hogarth Press, 1955

Freud S: The Ego and the Id (1923), in The Standard Edition of the Complete Psychological Works of Sigmund Freud, Vol 18. Translated and edited by Strachey J. London, Hogarth Press, 1955

Heimann P: On Countertransference. Int J Psychoanal 31:110–130, 1950

Klein M: Contributions to Psychoanalysis 1921–1945. Edited by Sutherland JD. London, Hogarth Press, 1968

Kohut H: The Analysis of the Self: A Systematic Approach to the Psychoanalytic Treatment of Narcissistic Personality Disorders. New York, International Universities Press, 1971

Kohut H: The Restoration of the Self. New York, International Universities Press, 1977

Mahler MS, Pine F, Bergman A: The Psychological Birth of the Human Infant. New York, Basic Books, 1975

Racker H: Transference and Counter-Transference. New York, International Universities Press. 1968

Modern Classics

Altshuler KZ: Psychotherapy 1945–95, in Review of Psychiatry, edited by Oldham JM, Riba MB. Washington, DC, American Psychiatric Press, 1994, pp 55–72

Ehrenwald J (ed): The History of Psychotherapy. Northvale, NJ, Jason Aronson, 1991

Ellenberger HF: The Discovery of the Unconscious: The History and Evolution of Dynamic Psychiatry. New York, Basic Books, 1970

Fairbairn WRD: Psychoanalytic Studies of the Personality. London, Routledge & Kegan Paul, 1952

Greenspan SI: The Development of the Ego: Implications for Personality Theory, Psychopathology and the Psychotherapeutic Process. New York, International Universities Press, 1989

Herman JL: Trauma and Recovery: The Aftermath of Violence—From Domestic Abuse to Political Terror. New York, Basic Books, 1942

Kernberg OF: Borderline Conditions and Pathological Narcissism. New York, Jason Aronson, 1975

Stern DN: The Interpersonal World of the Infant: A View from Psychoanalysis and Developmental Psychology. New York, Basic Books, 1985

Stolorow RD, Brandschaft B, Atwood GE: Psychoanalytic Treatment: An Intersubjective Approach. Hillsdale, NJ, Analytic Press, 1987

Terr L: Too Scared to Cry. New York, Basic Books, 1990

GLOSSARY

Abstinence   The therapist's technical stance of being somewhat silent, although not withholding, in order to better observe how the patient organizes his or her psychic world. Requires explanation to and education of the patient.

Acting out   The expression of unconscious conflict in action rather than words.

Behavior   Thoughts (cognitions), feelings (affects), fantasies, and actions.

Brief psychodynamic psychotherapy   A psychodynamic psychotherapy that is focal and of limited duration, usually 12 to 20 sessions.

Boundaries   The rules of interpersonal relating between patient and therapist that represent the best therapeutic environment for the patient and protect the patient from exploitation.

Case manager   The individual with whom the physician and patient maintain contact to obtain approval of reimbursement for planned care.

Complementary countertransference   The therapist's identification with a significant figure from the patient's past whom the patient is experiencing in the transference.

Concordant countertransference   The therapist's identification with the patient's emotional experience.

Countertransference   The psychotherapist's emotional experience of the patient. May be a help or an impediment to treatment. May be experienced by the therapist as pressure to act in a certain way with the patient. See also *complementary countertransference* and *concordant countertransference.*

Day residue   The part of the recent life experience used as the building block for a dream.

Defense   See *mechanisms of defense.*

Drive theory   A theoretical perspective in psychoanalysis that focuses on early childhood wishes (libidinal and aggressive) as the primary organizers of personality.

Ego psychology   A theoretical perspective in psychoanalysis that focuses on the role of the ego as mediator of wishes and prohibitions, on defense mechanisms and on non–conflict-related parts of the personality.

End phase of treatment   The stage of treatment that usually begins with setting the termination date. Patient is carrying on self-analysis, and the issues of ending and loss, as well as independence, are prominent. See also *termination.*

Evaluation phase   Initial two to four sessions, used to assess the patient and reach a treatment decision.

Explorative psychotherapy   See *psychodynamic psychotherapy.*

Free association   Technical procedure of encouraging the patient to speak as freely as possible, suspending judgment, and to say whatever comes to mind. Always only a relative term. Requires education of the patient.

Insight-oriented psychotherapy   See *psychodynamic psychotherapy.*

Interpretation The technical procedure of making what is unconscious (i.e., out of the patient's awareness) conscious. May include linking the transference with a present experience and also with a past significant figure.

Long-term psychotherapy See *psychodynamic psychotherapy.*

Managed care A system for delivery of health care built on the active direction of care through approval of reimbursement for care by the health care insurance company and the case manager. See also *case manager.*

Mechanisms of defense Ways of thinking (cognitions) directed toward decreasing unpleasant affective states (anxiety) and maintaining unconscious conflicts out of awareness. Examples include intellectualization, repression, externalization, somatization, splitting, denial, and acting out.

Midphase of treatment The middle part of treatment, during which the patient and therapist work together to examine defenses and transference.

Neurosis Older term used in psychoanalytic writings to mean *internal conflict.*

Objects See *object relationships.*

Object relationships Internal world of "people" distinguished from the "real" person, since this is the experiential world of the patient, populated with meanings and perceptions rather than real events.

Object relations theory A theoretical perspective in psychoanalysis that focuses on early object relationships as a primary organizer of personality.

Opening phase of treatment Initial phase of treatment, usually directed to establishment of the therapeutic alliance, the patient's initial experience of great expectations and then disillusionment, the patient's learning free association, and the patient's education in the process of examining defenses and the transference.

Primary gain The relief of unpleasant affects (anxiety) that accompanies the use of defense mechanisms. See *secondary gain.*

Psychic reality The "internal world"—that is, unconscious perceptions based on the meanings of events rather than on the actual events. Derives from biological givens and developmental experience.

Psychoanalysis A psychotherapeutic treatment of great intensity, usually several years in length and directed at the elaboration of the patient's psychic reality and world of meaning through examination of the transference. Focuses on how these areas affect behavior. Term also used to describe the theory of mental functioning derived from this technique.

Psychoanalytic psychotherapy See *psychodynamic psychotherapy.*

Psychodynamic evaluation The process of assessing the patient for psychodynamic psychotherapy. It includes 1) psychodynamic listening, 2) a mental status exam, 3) construction of a developmental history, including significant events, traumas, and developmental deficits, 4) identifying past and present wishes, defense mechanisms, important people, and self-esteem management and change, and 5) estimating the future doctor-patient relationship conflict areas (transference).

Psychodynamic listening A process of listening to the patient's history and present problems from the vantage point of the four psychologies of psychoanalysis (drive theory, ego psychology, object relations theory, and self psychology) and the subjective perspective of the patient's feeling world. In listening from the vantage point of the four psychologies, the psychiatrist listens to the patient's present function and past history of function and also develops hypotheses of past function based on present function and past history.

Psychodynamic psychotherapy (also called *psychoanalytic psychotherapy, insight-oriented psychotherapy, explorative psychotherapy, long-term psychotherapy*)   The talking cure, based on the principles of psychoanalytic understanding of mental functioning (e.g., presence of defenses, transference, and psychic reality) as aspects of mental life. The primary goal is to make what is out of awareness available for conscious processing through identifying patterns of behavior derived from childhood.

Psychotherapy   The generic term for all talking cures. Verbal interchange between an expert and a help seeker, the goal of which is to alter characteristic patterns of behavior that are causing the help seeker difficulties. Includes cognitive psychotherapy, interpersonal psychotherapy, and psychoanalysis, among others.

Resistance   The clinical term used to describe the therapist's experience of the patient's unconscious reluctance to experience disturbing affects related to childhood conflicts. Includes defense mechanisms, secondary gain, reinforcing nature of acting out, need to punish oneself, and need to thwart progress.

Secondary gain   Concrete advantages gained in reality from the presence of illness. See *primary gain.*

Self psychology   A theoretical perspective in psychoanalysis that focuses on the maintenance of the self, self-esteem, safety, and the early mother-child relationship, particularly the rapprochement phase of separation-individuation.

Supportive psychotherapy   Psychotherapy directed toward helping the patient reestablish his previous best level of functioning. The most common form of psychotherapy, requiring thoughtful and skilled application of psychodynamic principles and techniques.

Termination   The ending of psychotherapy. This phase is demanding for the therapist as well as the patient. See also *end phase of treatment.*

Therapeutic alliance   The reality-based relationship of the therapist and the patient working together.

Transference   Experience of acting, feeling, and/or perceiving another person to be like a significant figure from one's past. Important area of learning in the psychoanalytic psychotherapies, but not limited to therapy settings.

Transference resistance   Powerful wishes for transference gratification that may originate from positive or negative transference feelings.

Working alliance   See *therapeutic alliance.*

Subject Index

Page numbers printed in **boldface** *type refer to tables or figures.*

Author Index